Shoplifting

D1616424

Shoplifting

A Social History

by
KERRY SEGRAVE

McFarland & Company, Inc., Publishers
Jefferson, North Carolina, and London

Library of Congress Cataloguing-in-Publication Data

Segrave, Kerry, 1944–
    Shoplifting : a social history / by Kerry Segrave.
        p.   cm.
    Includes bibliographical references and index.
    ISBN 0-7864-0908-8 (softcover : 50# alkaline paper) ∞
    1. Shoplifting — History.   I. Title.
    HV6651.S44   2001
    364.16'2 — dc21   00-53707

British Library cataloguing data are available

Cover photograph by Marty McGee.

Manufactured in the United States of America

McFarland & Company, Inc., Publishers
  Box 611, Jefferson, North Carolina 28640
  www.mcfarlandpub.com

CONTENTS

PREFACE

This book looks at the activity of shoplifting over the last 140 years. It looks at the types of people singled out as the principal offenders and at retailers' ambivalent response to the activity, from selective prosecution to the utilization of high tech antitheft devices, to suing shoplifters to recover costs. Also examined are media accounts which have often used exaggerated numbers when discussing the activity, and the effect of private, corporate justice on the offense.

Back in the 1860s the typical shoplifter was from the lower classes and was basically a snatch-and-grab artist who stole from under the eyes of the store owner. By 1900 it was an upper class woman who shoplifted from a huge department store because she was a kleptomaniac. In the 1960s it was teenagers stealing — for kicks, on a dare. Whoever it was though, it was always somebody who believed literally in the concept that one did not pay retail.

Chapter 1

THE KLEPTOMANIAC STEALS THE SPOTLIGHT, 1860s–1918

"The rich have kleptomania, while the poor are taken down with larceny."—Unnamed New York City store executive, 1878

"the women with a mania for stealing ... the acute result of the temptation exercised on them by the department stores."—Emile Zola, 1883

Shoplifting is a practice that has been engaged in for centuries. Reports of theft from stalls and shops appeared in Elizabethan England. One of the earliest known accounts of shoplifting, penned in 1597, described the activities of a professional troupe. Daniel Defoe's fictional Moll Flanders was sent to Newgate Prison for shoplifting in mid-seventeenth century London. Another London, England, account stated that in the summer of 1726 shoplifters became so common, and so hard on retailers' profits, that the owners applied to the government for help in apprehending offenders. In nineteenth century America "light-fingered Sophie Lyons," a well known shoplifter, became a detective story heroine and wrote an autobiography that was syndicated by the Hearst newspaper chain.[1]

For the most part, though, the activity was sporadic and infrequent. It was after the Civil War that the prevalence and perception of shoplifting became significant enough to move the practice to the status of a serious and persistent problem. At the start of this period, offenders often worked in teams and often were male. Females had an advantage over males—one they would maintain for decades—in that female fashion afforded a lot of spacious hiding places for articles. Women carried purses of various sizes, wore outfits with long voluminous skirts, and were often decked out in shawls, gloves and muffs.

The social class of these offenders in the period immediately following the Civil War was mostly lower. Perpetrators were usually part of the criminal lower class who engaged in much petty criminal behavior, of which shoplifting was just one facet. They operated in a manner not unlike that of Moll Flanders two centuries earlier and an ocean away.

That so many of these early pilferers operated in teams was a function of retailing practices of the time. Shops were small and usually staffed by the owner who kept a wary eye on his premises and all those within it, which was possible due to the small physical size of the shop. Goods were not on open display. In order to see the hat that had caught one's eye the customer had to ask the owner, who retrieved it from behind a counter or barrier of some kind. Drastic changes were then underway in retailing which would largely be in place by the turn of the century. Those changes would dramatically alter the prevalence, practice, and perception of shoplifting. However, in the 1860s, those changes had had no real impact.

On December 27, 1863, Peter Hefferman (alias Peter Dunn, alias James Johnson) and his wife were arrested and charged with grand larceny, stealing watches and jewelry from the store of a Mr. Bronte. Already well known to the police, the Heffermans attracted the attention of police officer Timothy Golden when they were coming out of their residence in the morning. Golden followed them, saw them enter Bronte's, followed them to several other places, saw them enter a saloon, followed them in and arrested them. He found a box containing the watches and jewelry in Hefferman's pocket. After Hefferman was found guilty, a report commented, "The conviction of this man disposes of one of the most successful shoplifters that has been known in this country for years. The prisoner and his wife possessed the advantages of genteel address, respectable appearance and great shrewdness and are reported to have accumulated a fortune by thievery and shoplifting."[2]

Mary Brown, alias Frances Stanley "an expert shoplifter," pled guilty in June 1865 to a charge of grand larceny (shoplifting) for stealing from a store. Brown had only recently been released from state prison after serving 4½ years for a similar offence.[3]

After receiving several complaints of shoplifters operating in stores in the Canal Street area of New York, Captain Irving of the detective squad set out in February 1874 to stop the offenders. Irving and his partner toured the area where they saw Mary Moore, alias "Long Mary, a well-known shoplifter," come out of a store. They followed her into a saloon where they arrested her. When apprehended, said one account, "She took from under her skirts a large linen bag, such as is usually worn by professional shoplifters, and handed it to Capt. Irving. The bag was found to contain several boxes of kid gloves, ten boxes of mohair braids and several other articles valued in all at $180 which she had stolen from the store in Walker Street, while examining the stock under the pretense of desiring to make purchases." Long Mary was also described as "one of the adroitest shoplifters in the City."[4]

About one year later "a notorious shop-lifter" by the name of Christina Meyer was arrested on a charge of stealing a piece of silk worth $80 from the store of Lord and Taylor. She was assisted by two men and a woman, all of whom escaped. In the rooms where the four lived, police found a large quantity of property consisting of valuable shawls, ladies' underwear, spoons, knives, forks, beadwork and three pawn tickets for gold watches. The men had each served five-year prison terms, for shoplifting.[5]

In January 1876 Julien Blum, Moses Leon, and Morris Klein entered the store of Henry Shaw at different times and met outside after reconnoitering the place. Blum pretended that he wanted to purchase linen. They were noticed by two detectives who regarded their movements as suspicious and determined to watch them. On the following day the three men returned to the store and upon leaving the shop were arrested and searched. On the persons of Klein and Leon were found four pieces of Belfast linen, stolen from Shaw's store and valued at $140. Blum was found guilty at trial and sentenced to five years in state prison. The 77-year old Klein pled guilty, claiming he had been driven to the deed by poverty. He was sentenced to three years, "in consideration of his age." Out on bail, Leon had skipped town.[6]

Mary Ann Watts, alias Mary Wilson, a "clever" shoplifter, was convicted of larceny in December 1873 and sentenced to three years in Sing Sing. Three months later she escaped. Spotted by police in April 1876, then calling herself Mary Walker, she was arrested by police. Apprehended with her was her friend Annie Smith. A search of the pair resulted in the finding of a number of stolen items on Smith and 85 yards of silk in a wallet concealed under Watt's overskirt.[7]

The prevalence of shoplifting was increasing. In 1876 in Boston, Detectives Wood and Wiggin were watching especially for shoplifters. On one day they arrested Mary Brett and Mary Brown for shoplifting at the stores of Whitney and Stearns on Tremont Street. Goods valued at $20 were found on the person of each. The pair were arraigned and fined an unreported amount. On the following day the two detectives greeted a train arriving from New York City and arrested the disembarking Mollie Hoye, Sarah Clifford, and Mary Wilson, alias Frenchy Johnson, said to be "three of the most expert and notorious shoplifters to be found in this or any other country." They were put on a return train to New York a couple of hours later. Later that same day the pair of detectives picked up Tilly Miller and Lena Nugent, alias Black Lena. Both women were wanted in Brooklyn after escaping from jail, where they had been placed for shoplifting offenses.[8]

A Fulton Street, Brooklyn, firm which sold hats and furs reported to the police in January 1877 that they had lost at different times during the previous six months a number of valuable sacques—a woman's loose-fitting jacket or cape. Assigned to the case, Detectives Corwin and Looney learned that on the day the last sacque disappeared "a well-dressed, lady-like young girl" had been seated in the store for some time, on the pretense she was waiting for her brother, who had promised to meet her there and buy her a sacque. Store employees thought she had been in the store on one ruse or another several times. Corwin and Looney then started a search of the pawnshops, finally locating the sacque in question, along with a good description of the owner. Eventually they arrested Sarah Redmond who confessed she had been shoplifting for a long time. At her home a quantity of stolen items were found; on her person were 75 pawn tickets.[9]

That same year Rosa Rode and a male companion entered a store on Broadway in New York where the man priced some items while Rosa "lounged about the store." An employee saw the woman hide a box under her shawl. When the pair left the shop the employee followed them and summoned the police. Rosa was arrested but the male escaped. She was found to have seven dozen pairs of kid gloves hidden under her shawl and in her felt petticoat was an "immense pocket" which held two boxes containing nine more dozen pairs of kid gloves. Those 16 dozen pairs were valued at $140. She was held for trial in lieu of $5,000 bail. One week later she pled guilty and was sentenced to 3½ years in jail. This case illustrated the advantage females had over males in stashing goods on their persons. Rosa had managed to secrete almost 200 pairs of gloves on her person and almost got away with it. Even at this early period most of the shoplifters' tricks, such as the booster bag to receive pilfered items, hidden within one's clothing, were already well known and well used.[10]

Rosa did her time but was not long on the streets before again running afoul of the law. It was reported in April 1880 that Mary Scanlan, alias Rosy Roder—known as Kid Glove Rosie—and Louisa Rice were "two notorious pickpockets" arrested in the act of stealing 180 yards of silk from a Broadway store. Both had prior shoplifting convictions. Scanlan chose a trial while Rice pled guilty. The judge noted that the large dry goods establishments in New York suffered great losses by the depredations of shoplifters and he was determined to administer severe punishment to all offenders brought before him. Scanlan received five years, "the full penalty," while Rice received four years and nine months—in consideration of having pled guilty she had three months taken off.[11]

Even then, Christmas was a popular time for shoplifting. It was easier to pilfer when the streets and stores were jammed. On December 24, 1877, Detective Lenahan was patrolling Brooklyn's Fulton Street. His suspicions were aroused by a woman who was in and out of many stores. Lenahan followed her but could spot no crime. Nonetheless Lenahan arrested Mary Mason, alias Catherine Connor, as she got off a streetcar. On her person she was found to have six pairs of kid gloves, three silk handkerchiefs, two bottles of cologne, a pair of bracelets, and a cigar holder in a morocco case. At her residence more stolen items were found.[12]

During the 1870s a transition began to take place in shoplifting reports. More and more it came to be viewed as a crime committed solely by women. At least partly this was due to the beginnings of mass retailing to a mass consumer base, in huge premises. Shopping was set up to attract primarily women. A second difference taking place at this time was that more and more women arrested for the offense were well-to-do, of good character. That is, they were not lower class. This phenomenon would lead to a major change in how the justice system would deal with those accused of shoplifting. It was one thing to sentence a lower class woman to many years in prison for shoplifting—as happened all the time. However, it was unthinkable that this would be done to upper class women. For that matter it was unthinkable that well-to-do women, whose only trouble with the law was shoplifting, would be treated like common criminals at all, notwithstanding that all lower class women so charged were so treated. Out of this difficulty was born the concept of kleptomania.

In the summer of 1876 a "fashionably-dressed" lady entered a store and inquired about the price of several bronzes. Just after she left, the clerk noticed a $45 statuette of Mercury was missing. He chased after her and had her arrested by a police officer who found the item on her person. Initially she was held on $1,000 bail. A day later that was reduced to $500 when a man arrived to make an affidavit to her good character. She was released on bail.[13]

Emma Deming was arrested on Christmas Eve 1880 in the store of B. Altman and Co. for shoplifting a bottle of cologne. When arrested she had the cologne on her person along with a small valise containing three pocketbooks, all identified as property of the firm. At the time of her arrest she offered to pay for the cologne but the offer was refused. Deming explained she could not remember whether or not she had left money on the counter to pay for the cologne, but she had intended to. She further explained she found the valise on the floor, picked it up and while searching for the owner was suddenly arrested. At her trial witnesses testified to her good character. B. Altman indicated they were willing to withdraw the complaint. In the end, "the court declared that the good character of the prisoner strengthened the doubt it had entertained at the outset as to her guilt, and rendered a verdict of acquittal."[14]

Similar problems were happening in Europe. In Paris, France, during June 1877 the trial of three foreigners from Venezuela on shoplifting charges took place. The defendants were persons of "good families, Mrs. Pulgar, wife of a former general and representative of Venezuela in Paris, her niece Ms. Lopez, and the latter's husband." The women were described as "elegantly dressed, of attractive and distinguished appearance." This financially well-to-do trio was arrested after the theft of a sapphire ring at a store. A search of their apartment turned up a great quantity of stolen goods. Their method of operation was for Pulgar and Mr. Lopez to occupy the attention of the employees while the other woman "laid hands on anything near her." The young woman got eight months in jail while the other two were each sentenced to a year and a day. Usually the wealthy never reached court on shoplifting charges—they paid their way out of trouble. However, a minority of retailers pursued a prosecute-all policy, in the belief that was the only way to reduce the practice. In that case, and assuming a judge was determined to be fair and not class-biased (not always true), upper class women ran the risk of prison time. That prospect made kleptomania even more inviting as a saving strategy.[15]

The existence of gangs of professional shoplifters was already noted by the 1870s. Extensive shoplifting operations against dry good stores in Cleveland led to the arrests of six people, described as a gang of shoplifters from Chicago. A search warrant executed at a house used by the group led to the discovery of hundreds of dollars of goods, including silk handkerchiefs, laces, whole pieces of silk, and so forth.[16]

Also by this time false arrests of people were taking place, with a resultant fear on the part of retailers of being sued for damages by wrongfully accused shoppers. A Mrs. Davis was awarded $150 in damages in 1878 after being wrongfully accused of shoplifting a purse from a New York store. She was forcibly detained by the store and searched as a result of the accusation. The New York Times editorialized that while a "system of somewhat suspicious watchfulness" was necessary in stores, a little more care could be exercised in selecting store detectives. "Instances of consummate ability on the part of detectives in the higher walks of their profession are sufficiently rare; among the astute persons who dog the steps of suspected visitors in front of shop-counters, hopeless stupidity seems to be disagreeably prevalent. A little more care in the selection of this kind of talent would help greatly to popularize certain stores."[17]

Later that same year Ellen Whalen found herself in court charged with stealing an item of clothing from a dry goods store. Store detective Alexander Sisson testified he saw Whalen take the item from the counter and conceal it under her cloak. He followed her out of the store, brought her back and locked her in the basement of the shop until police arrived. Whalen's lawyer got Sisson to admit he didn't know if the item had or had not been sold to the accused. Proof was produced by the defense that Whalen purchased the item whereupon she was discharged.[18]

Catherine Walsh, "an elderly respectable-looking woman," was charged with shoplifting in 1880. A store clerk testified she saw the accused take 85 cents worth of sleeve buttons and hide them in her shawl. Walsh was approached by the clerk's boss who demanded the buttons's return. Hotly denying the charge, Walsh nevertheless later gave the buttons back to the clerk saying they must have fallen accidentally into the folds of her shawl. Charged anyway, Walsh was convicted and fined $25. Noted a reporter, "Although the offense was, in itself, a trivial one, the result of the trial, by reason of the certainty of a suit for damages in the event of an acquittal, was looked forward to with much interest by proprietors of Broadway establishments, many of whom were in court."[19]

The confusion between employee theft and shoplifting happened on occasion. Both contributed to a retailer's overall loss, known in the trade as "shrinkage." However, they were separate issues, although the entire shrinkage figure was often attributed solely to shoplifting — in the old days and in current times. When 18-year-old Lizzie Creamer, an $8 a week salesclerk employed by dry goods merchant Hartung & Co., was caught stealing items while she was on duty, she was charged and convicted of shoplifting — and sentenced to 60 days in prison. The newspaper report headed the item "Found Guilty of Shop-Lifting."[20]

By the end of the 1870s, shoplifting in Paris was characterized as "very commonplace.... Every week we hear of arrests for petty larcenies, and in many cases the criminals are ladies of family and position." Two such American women escaped their predicament by paying for the lifted items and by giving $100 to the poor. It was said, "Kleptomania seems to be on the increase." Also arrested was a wealthy German countess: "She confessed that her mania for pocketing small things was so strong that she was unable to resist it, and she offered to pay any sum not to be exposed." The store owners countered that they had tried the lenient approach for a long and an unsuccessful time and now felt they had to take a more severe approach. The countess was charged. More generally it was reported that "all the great shops have to employ special detectives, and men are kept watching through holes in the ceiling. Every week several ladies are caught, but thus far a majority have been able to compromise with the proprietor for a large sum of money."[21]

By then kleptomania was also a defense in American courts. Emma Parsons shoplifted $5 worth of items from a dry goods shop late in 1879. She had more than enough money on her to pay for the goods. Her lawyer entered a plea of "temporary insanity or kleptomania." Parsons was established to be of "good character" with her brother testifying that she was "peculiarly characterized by stupidity." When the accused took the stand she admitted taking the items but claimed she didn't know why. The jury declared: "We acquit her of any intention to steal."[22]

Shoplifting had become so prevalent by 1878 in New York that the *Times* did a general round-up article, including interviews with several department store executives, albeit all unnamed. One such retailer mentioned that unfortunately his store sometimes arrested an innocent person by mistake. It was regarded as extremely unpleasant for a businessman to have anyone arrested in his store, even a professional thief. It injured the business in this way: "Respectable ladies, reading in the newspapers of the arrest of shoplifters in stores, sometimes on suspicion, grow nervous over the chance, which is a slim one, that they may be mistaken for thieves, and put to the indignity of being taken to a Police station. Many ladies have said to me, 'Mr. Blank, I am almost afraid to come into your store, for fear of being arrested.'" He added that in former times there were no store detectives employed since there were no large establishments. In such establishments the owner and any clerks could see all over the place, and they called a police officer when they found anybody stealing. In the large and crowded department stores, already in place in 1878, it was impossible for busy clerks to also watch over the stock. When this executive talked of gender differences in shoplifting he touched on an obvious point, but one that few others made. "As a very large proportion of our customers are ladies, it would be unfair to say, from the experience of any dry goods or fancy goods house, that women are more apt to steal than men. The people arrested here are all women, of course, but then we have hardly any male customers. Even if we had, there is nothing here that they would care for."[23]

Compare those remarks with the ones from the superintendent of a second department store "...stealing seems to come natural to a great many women.... We sometimes think that some people like to steal where they are closely watched, just to convince themselves of their shrewdness, and gloat over it in private." From an executive with a third store came the estimate that one woman in nine who entered his store was a professional thief, one in nine was an amateur thief who entered the premises with the fixed idea of taking a particular item, and one in nine came with no fixed intent but spontaneously took something which caught her attention. Six of nine women entering his store would not steal, he thought. One large dry goods store was then estimating its annual loss from petty thievery at $10,000. While kleptomania was catching on as a defense with the accused and with the courts and those in the psychiatric field it never did have much credence with retailing personnel, not with executives, owners, clerks, or store detectives. Said the above-mentioned superintendent, "There may be such a thing as kleptomania, but it is difficult to detect it. It is rather a just criticism that the rich have kleptomania, while the poor are taken down with larceny. I hardly think there is such a disease, but, undoubtedly, there is a mania among some people to steal."[24]

Arrests for shoplifting exceeded 4,000 in Paris, France, in 1883. Most of those were described as not belonging to the "needy classes." Here, a simple bribe was the quickest way out. Noted one account, "As a rule, the shopkeepers hand over the shoplifters to the Commissary of Police, but not infrequently they drop the case on the payment of a heavy fine 'for the relief of the poor.'" For example, one wealthy woman who shoplifted 65 francs worth of articles was told she would not be prosecuted if she made a contribution of 1,000 francs to poverty relief.[25]

By 1883 a reporter noted about shoplifting that: "The evil prevails everywhere in mercantile circles, but it is most oppressingly felt by those firms that conduct the large retail emporiums which are crowded with customers most of the time. Such establishments as occupy whole blocks, or large portions of blocks, and invite a miscellaneous patronage by dealing in a great variety of articles, are the ones that principally suffer from the depredations of shoplifters." It was then reported that in a dozen of the largest retail stores, owners estimated their annual losses to shoplifting at $8,000 to $12,000 each. Kleptomania drew a great amount of space in this report, described as an "evil" familiar to all shopkeepers. Acknowledging that some retailers professed to believe there was such a disorder, the reporter encountered many more whose lips "curled sarcastically" at the mention of the word: "Kleptomania? Oh, you mean the excuse that people of good social standing give when they are caught stealing." Generally, retailers were said to be averse to taking notice of small thefts by females of wealth and high social standing "and they frequently let them go unpunished rather than stir up the excitement that always follows the accusation of a woman." Even professional female thieves were said to have no trouble in arousing the sympathies of bystanders whenever they were detected and openly charged with the commission of theft, and whenever a "real lady" was thus accused the feeling which arose against the store owner was intense.[26]

One owner of a large retail store commented; "The meanest phase of this whole shoplifting business is what you call kleptomania. It is something that we cannot touch without making a mess of it, and we are compelled to look quietly on from day to day and see ourselves robbed, not only by people of eminent respectability, but by some of our best customers." He added that he didn't believe in kleptomania, and of all the shoplifting cases he had dealt with, "I have not seen one which appeared to me to have an innocent or unconscious larceny." Rather, he felt, American women were gradually acquiring the habit of pilfering and that females of social position did not scruple to steal small things. Like most owners this man didn't feel like driving a good customer away by proving her to be a thief, unless her stealing amounted to enough to cause the store a serious loss. "And when we are forced to take steps to stop such pilferings we are met by tears and reproaches and the ever-ready excuse of 'kleptomania,' with an indignant reminder from the accused person's relatives and friends of her 'highly respectable position in society.'" Professional shoplifters had also been in the habit of affecting the "kleptomania dodge" when apprehended but since retailers had become so exacting in their demands for "proofs of good character in such cases the thieves have abandoned that subterfuge." Store owners were then in the habit, in the case of known shoplifters, of reporting their description to other stores. When a different store owner was asked what proportion of shoplifters were female he replied, "Fully nineteen-twentieths. It is seldom that a male shoplifter attempts to work a retail store alone, and the instances where women are assisted by men are not frequent." Store detectives were sometimes ex-police officers but more frequently they were experienced salespeople, usually men. Long service enabled them to become familiar with faces. Among the large retail premises in uptown New York in 1883 it was reported that "there are not more than one in four that employ regular detectives all of the time."[27]

Macy and Co. had a female store detective, Mary Plunkett, who started work with the retailer in 1879, becoming a store detective in 1888. Seven years later she estimated she had been involved in over 100 shoplifting arrests. She did not believe in kleptomania, stating, "Women I give into custody I class as dishonest." Explaining Macy's policy of dealing with people apprehended for shoplifting Plunkett commented: "It is not generally known, perhaps, that in the case of a detected person, who denies, blusters and threatens there is no 'let-up,' while in that of a person who at once breaks down, tells her name and address promptly, confesses and exhibits the penitence of a novice, the firm never prosecutes. Such a penitent receives a word of advice or caution, the terms of which admit of no doubt, not to enter the store again, and — freedom. We have quite a number of them."[28]

An example of the kind of fuss sometimes created when a woman was arrested could be seen in 1905 when store detective John Larkin apprehended a well-dressed, middle-aged woman in a large department store. She responded by "fighting and screaming, trying to jab her hatpin into her captor." This caused a crowd of patrons in the store to gather "threateningly" around Larkin, as they did not know the woman was under arrest. When he took her outside into the street to be sent to the police station she screamed out noisily with the result that another crowd swarmed around Larkin. While this woman had stolen items worth $3.50 she had on her person $400. Larkin said he had arrested the same woman two years earlier on the same charge and that she was released "after he had been urged to show mercy by a son and daughter, who appeared to be persons of wealth."[29]

Some $500,000 of goods was said to be shoplifted annually from New York stores, in 1906, "by professional shoplifters, professional kleptomaniacs of aristocratic birth, and persons who take things because they are in sore need." Lawyer Mark Alter, who had defended over 500 people accused of shoplifting (all women) said that of the 4,000 arrests each year for the offence only about 700 made it into court and of that number not more than 50 were convicted. "Many women present the plea of an unseen and supernatural force which impels them to steal," he added. Shoplifters were usually not accused in the store, but followed outside first. Next they would be taken to an office in the store and questioned closely. If it was decided to release the accused without further prosecution, that person was required to sign an agreement releasing the store from all liabilities from damage suits, a precaution said to be necessary "because of the many persons who from time to time have made a point of appearing guilty without really being so, and when accused, have made trouble for the proprietors."[30]

Christmas had become such an active time for shoplifters by the turn of the century that many of the larger retailers employed extra detectives. On one December day in 1907, two detectives employed in one department store arrested six people for the offence, all in separate incidents. One woman explained to her captors: "A woman friend told me to do it. She said that she and her friends took little things in the stores, and never were caught. Besides, she told me that if I were caught I should get only a lecture and a warning."[31]

That same month on one day in court 30 people appeared on shoplifting charges, all from separate incidents. Most were paroled. However, one was sentenced to 20 days for stealing lace handkerchiefs.[32]

So common was the offence that in 1908 Leslie Graff, secretary of the Retail Dry Goods Association of New York City, declared "war" on shoplifters. Having stood the drain as long as they could, this merchants' trade group announced that every case of shoplifting henceforth detected would be vigorously prosecuted. Every retailer said likely to suffer from shoplifting was represented in the group. Also, the district attorney had agreed to cooperate in obtaining convictions. This may have been one of the first times such a pronouncement was made, but it would not be the last. The declaration that all those apprehended would be prosecuted was never put into practice. Graff explained that the explicit understanding was that when once a case of shoplifting was detected the matter passed completely out of the hands of the owners of the store where the theft took place, and they would have no right to interfere with the prosecution. Supposedly that would end the practice whereby people apprehended in a store pleaded with the proprietor with tears streaming down their cheeks, and often were dealt with leniently. Under Graff's plan that could not happen as the merchants themselves would be helpless since prosecution passed to the State and to the Retail Dry Goods Association legal staff. As to who was doing the shoplifting Graff said: "The professional shoplifters don't bother us much ... nor is it the poor people who rob the stores, in most cases. Wives of prominent business men, wives of clergymen, well-to-do supposedly respectable women whose husbands make from $5,000 to $15,000 a year are those who prey upon the stores. They don't need to take the things; they just take them, and when they are detected and brought before the proprietors of the store they weep and beg for mercy. They say their husbands will leave them if they find it out, and usually the merchants let the matter pass. They will not do so in the future."[33]

At another retailer, a store detective commented that his establishment didn't fear professional thieves, nor the poor people who stole from need. Rather, "the dangerous ones are the rich and influential women who either yield to a temporary impulse of temptation or are afflicted with a sort of degenerate tendency towards kleptomania. Some of the women that I have caught — and let go often enough — had accounts at the shop and all the money they needed." The reporter interviewing the detective went on to describe the scene of customers in a fashionable department store by saying, "It seems impossible that these beautifully gowned, gracefully moving creatures, all polish and delicacy and poise, should harbor among them all one single thief." He went on to add, "The word seems absurd, an affront to their well-bred faces and their well-filled purses dangling on jeweled chains. And yet it is indeed from this class that the army of shoplifters is largely made-up — this rich, well-mannered, well-nurtured crowd of fair, fine ladies, who order $200 worth of purchases in a morning with a nonchalant 'Charge to my account and send to-day.'"[34]

Methods of shoplifting have changed little in the past hundred years. At the start of the 1900s one method was to try on new clothes, such as coats and dresses, and walk out wearing them, leaving the old, and worthless, behind. Another method was to look at lace items, scarves for example, accumulate a big pile, and then try and secrete one or more items away, perhaps in a muff or jacket. One woman had a hollow heel fashioned in her shoes, another had puffs of hair lacquered to extra stiffness, to act as a receptacle for small items. Some women used unbuttoned shirtwaists to stow goods in, or inside low shoes, or up the openings of gloves. Items were also transported in the armpit, the muff, bag, or coat. One woman made off with a $200 silk gown. She had rolled the gown up and carried it off held between her knees, walking only with the lower part of her legs. At one leading retailer the detective estimated that, combined, New York City's leading shops lost $1 million per year to shoplifting. Yet he still let many of those he apprehended go without further prosecution. Those released had to fill out a form, a sort of confessional, which was then kept in the store's safe. Usually they were also told to never enter the store again. Regarding the mechanics of the arrest procedure the detective observed, "I always take up the people myself and unless I see them steal, and I see them acting suspiciously later, I let them go. We'd rather lose hundreds of dollars than make one big mistake and expose ourselves to a suit. And we never arrest them in the shop."[35]

London, England, was experiencing the same type of problem in its fashionable West End retailing district. Said the manager of a department store located there; "One million dollars a year is the price the merchants have to pay for displaying their goods so attractively … every arrest entails publicity, and no reputable establishment likes to have it become known that it is a frequent prey of the shoplifters. It might keep good customers away. We prefer, if possible, to keep the thieves away. This is comparatively easy with the amateur who is caught committing her first offense. She usually belongs to a respectable family, and readily promises never to enter the store again if she can escape the shame of arrest and trial." A problem was that the first offender group kept being replenished. Why? This manager commented, "Perhaps, too, the spread of Socialism has something to do with it. People are coming to believe that they have just as much right to the luxuries of life as their more wealthy neighbor and they start out to get them without any misgivings as to the moral aspect of the method."[36]

London shop owners had united to fight their own war against shoplifters. Blacklists had been drawn up and circulated to other retailers with all the clerks ordered not to give service to the people on the lists. That was a preventive measure but the real problem lay in suppression of a practice which, noted one account, "when aired in the publicity of a court is certain to cause business to suffer as it is generally believed that honest customers avoid a shop which is known to take unusual precautions against delinquents and always punishes them when caught." Methods used by English shoplifters included utilizing a bag with a false bottom, a garter with a row of hooks, a hole through a skirt which allowed the passage of goods into a secret pocket in the underskirt, dropping small articles down the back of the neck while ostensibly arranging the hair. A more elaborate method involved placing wax under the edge of a jewelry counter. Then the customer would examine items, discretely sticking an item such as a ring on the wax. Deciding not to buy anything the customer left the store. If apprehended, a search would of course yield nothing. Later a confederate would make a trivial purchase at the counter and retrieve the items. Also utilized were the hollow book, jewelry hidden in the hair and even a secret pocket in the collar of a pet dog. Such animals were taught to "stray" out of the shop and go home.[37]

Not long before World War I began Boston District Attorney Joseph Pelletier declared that shoplifting cost each of the large department stores of that city an average of $50,000 annually. He recommended that merchants protect their goods with glass cases or wire screens.[38]

By the last decade of the 1800s shoplifting was a serious problem, occurring mainly in department stores. Some store managers claimed the loss of goods to shoplifters was largely the result of indifferent or inattentive sales clerks, "some of whom lounged behind the counters as though propping up a fixture." Retailers began to overcome their initial reluctance to prosecute offenders. Penalties were severe in Canada, as they were in the United States at this time. A Markham, Ontario, woman and her daughter were sent to prison for 6 to 18 months for theft from the Eaton's store. Another offender was sentenced to seven days in prison for shoplifting a six cent comb from the same retailer. In 1897 the Eaton's assistant superintendent was sworn in as a special constable and given the power to arrest suspects upon the store premises. A few years later profound disagreement broke out over the question of whether floorwalkers had the power to apprehend those believed to be shoplifters. As in America, the Eaton firm extracted written confessions from those they apprehended, along with promises to not enter the premises again, if they released them without further prosecution. When children were involved they were taken home to their parents.[39]

During that same decade in France the situation became so serious that retailers obliged inspectors to divide their duties between disciplining employees (for not being attentive enough to theft) and policing the clientele. The Bon Marche went so far as to offer employees a 10 franc bonus and two evenings off for signaling to an inspector that a theft was taking place.[40]

As discussed above, the size of department stores created a significant change in shopping. It meant the shop was way too big for an owner to monitor. More and more that task fell to clerks, who didn't have the same interest in apprehending suspects. Additionally, the move to huge shopping areas demanded an equally large pool of customers milling around. Consumption was, of course, crucial but the ambience and psychology of mass retailing required a mass of consumers who were at least browsing, if not buying. That made it harder for clerks to monitor customers. Eventually the problem was handled by retailers moving more and more to using in-store detectives, employees whose sole duties were to stop thefts. Another associated shopping change was the move to having most goods on open access display—compared to the previous method whereby one had to ask the owner or clerk to retrieve the item. Under open access it made it much more difficult to monitor items. When Henry G. Selfridge, Marshall Field & Co. general manager, established his American-style department store, with free entry for all, in London, England, in 1902 he was "severely censured" by London magistrates for his alleged encouragement of shoplifting in doing so.[41]

Just 10 years earlier a trade journal commented, "British dry-goods stores have no goods openly displayed or on counters... The bane of the American stores, the kleptomaniac, is scarcely known here and the force of floorwalkers and inspectors is correspondingly small." Crowds were important to the stores which actively encouraged them. Crowds had to be manufactured on a daily basis, to be themselves part of the allure of the stores. Women charged with shoplifting sometimes accused retailers of permitting too much freedom; they claimed they became "over excited" and excessively stimulated in the big stores. They could not refrain from handling items, they further argued, and no one in the store's employ stopped them. To them it was a "deplorable liberty" to touch everything. Many of these women shoppers were caught in the tension between traditional values, such as the postponement of gratification and the new command to consume. Department stores did their best to encourage as much impulse buying as possible. Retailers relied on their ability to break down self-control and rational behavior patterns. Shoppers—whether they bought or stole—were doing what was expected of them: succumbing to the siren call of the merchandise.[42]

This new method of mass retailing which developed in America from roughly the end of the Civil War—and was pervasive by 1920—was developed for women. As researcher Elaine Abelson wrote, shopping became increasingly understood as "the chief diversion of ladies." Shopping became something which both genders saw as being natural and innate as any other female physiological function. Within the Victorian world shopping became a natural public sphere for women. By 1904, R. H. Macy and Co. claimed it had 150,000 daily customers; estimates of the proportion of females in that number ranged as high as 90 percent. Males were not excluded but females were the primary consumers and it was to them specifically that department stores targeted their appeals. Free access within the stores was a major attraction. For the first time, noted Abelson, a woman could "circulate on her own, unattended, without interference from anyone and without rendering account to anyone." That freedom within the environment of the department store was not found in other areas of a woman's life. Child care was often provided within the store. It was a protected space where a woman could have tea, meet her friends, eat lunch, write a letter, rest, and browse. In 1902 one store declared, to its female customers, "You may roam our floors unquestioned, without being urged unduly to buy ... our place is to entertain you." In the 1990s one journalist looked back to say that the most important event in the history of shoplifting occurred in 1879 when F. W. Woolworth opened in Utica, New York, the first of what would become his five-and-ten stores. It was a radical idea: take the goods out of glass cabinets and display them where customers could select what they wanted themselves.[43]

The shoplifting which appeared suddenly in America in the late nineteenth century was entirely different from anything which had preceded it. Quickly it became the subject of medical concern and widespread popular interest. This shoplifting heralded a form of deviant behavior by a new group, the middle class. Its locale was cited in the new commercial institution—the department store—within the context of an expanding consumer capitalism. Additionally, it was linked to a strict gender role division that assigned consumption behavior to women. Under the label "kleptomania" it was used to define class- and gender-based notions of theft. It was taken for granted that this new offender—the middle class (or better) female accused of shoplifting—was legally and morally innocent as well as that her actions were compulsive. At least it was taken for granted by the medical and court officials who dealt with such women; the general public had more mixed views. Use of the diagnosis of kleptomania to defend and excuse the activities of a select group of women was evidence of the powerful role nineteenth century physicians played in orchestrating, shaping, and giving analytic visibility to sex-based definitions. It was also evidence of the socially sanctioned privilege of the white middle class in the nineteenth century.[44]

Quickly the female kleptomaniac became a popular joke, a stock character who appeared in sketches by comics such as Charlie Chaplin and Weber and Fields, as well as in countless vaudeville acts, drawing-room comedies and in popular songs such as "Mamie, Don't You Feel Ashamie." Edwin Porter's 1905 silent film "The Kleptomaniac" was just one of many film treatments of this new, and quickly ubiquitous, social phenomenon. Helping to fuel the hold on Victorian society by the kleptomaniac were two parallel developments in America in the last part of the nineteenth century. One was the singular importance the department store came to have as an urban institution; the second was the increasing status and authority of medical science. It was within this context that the figure of the kleptomaniac emerged.[45]

Precisely the same thing was happening at the same time in France. A growing and unprecedented number of stories appeared in the journals of French forensic medicine — individual histories of kleptomania, mostly women, diagnosed as stealing from compulsion. This trend was particularly pronounced after 1880 when, said researcher Patricia O'Brien, "The diagnosis became popular in a society marked by new consumer behavior in the marketplace." Psychiatry was then fighting to demonstrate its utility as expert testimony in the law courts. Forensic specialists, psychiatrists, lawyers, and department store owners joined forces in focusing an increasing amount of attention on what was considered an "epidemic" of stealing after 1880. There were no hard numbers on the offence; most went undetected. In official crime statistics, shoplifting was lumped together with all other types of theft. "More significantly, the stores, the courts, and the legal and medical professions sought to protect from public scrutiny many of the individuals arrested, especially if they were otherwise respectable bourgeois women. With kleptomania, protection was even more certain because of concern for the patient and her family's honor." General agreement existed on two points: that after 1880 shoplifting was dramatically different in extent and type from earlier retail theft and that between 1880 and 1920 shoplifting was sharply increasing. Criminologists were fascinated by the fact that shoplifting was a crime committed almost exclusively by women. The only other similar crime was that of prostitution.[46]

Kleptomania was "discovered" when the work of Swiss doctor Andre Matthey appeared in France in 1816. He defined *Klopemanie*— as he called it — as a type of theft that was monomaniacal due to the impulsive nature of the theft. While a diagnosis of stealing as a form of madness predated Matthey he was important in formulating a theory about certain behaviors. Although an amorphous medical term, monomania was meant to describe obsession or delirium with an object. Females who stole were sometimes released by the courts before 1816 for mental imbalance, but they did not have the benefit of a systematic judicial defense before the groundwork was laid by the Swiss physician.

The concept of kleptomania as a legal description for extenuating circumstances in the commission of a crime was developed further in 1840 by French physician C. C. Marc. He became the first to use the term "kleptomania," which he defined as "a distinctive, irresistible tendency to steal." Primarily he was concerned with the social position and background of the accused. He also placed an emphasis on females when he spoke of "certain secretions and excretions," such as milk and menstrual flow. As researcher Patricia O'Brien noted of this period, "It is safe to assert that if the patient was both bourgeois and female, certification as a kleptomaniac was a virtual certainty." In the case of a male accused, bourgeois origins coupled with the theft of an apparently useless object resulted in the same diagnosis.

Over the following 40 years others extended the concern with family history even further and publicized it with a more developed concept of hereditary mental degeneration. Kleptomania also came to be more explicitly seen, beginning around the 1880s, as another form of "hysterical behavior." In the latter part of the nineteenth century, most works on the topic coupled kleptomania exclusively with the newly created department stores. Men were more frequently mentioned in earlier works on the subject, although they remained a small minority both before and after mid–nineteenth century. In other ways, there was a similarity. Kleptomaniacs were always from bourgeois families who had engaged in stealing items they apparently did not need and should have been able to pay for. The number of cases proliferated dramatically.[47]

Beginning with an article by Charles Lasegue in 1879, French psychiatrists began to draw a connection between impulsive stealing and the "grands magasins." What struck them was the growing number of kleptomaniacs arrested in department stores and the fact that so few of these women were incited to steal elsewhere. A Dr. Lacassagne wrote, "Women of all sorts, drawn to these elegant surroundings by instincts native to their sex, fascinated by so many rash provocations, dazzled by the abundance of trinkets and lace, find themselves overtaken by a sudden, unpremeditated, almost savage impulse." He cautioned that "the department stores make great profits.... However the prosperity of these colossal enterprises must not take place at the expense of public morality." This was still, after all, said another writer of that era, a time when women were entrusted with "a noble mission in society." Paul Dubuisson, the forensic specialist for France's Tribunal of the Seine noted that "women find these [department stores] a milieu where whatever they possess in the way of moral staying power can no longer protect them, whereas they defend themselves successfully in all other settings."[48]

Dubuisson sought to demonstrate the existence of "that special folly which seizes a woman the moment she crosses the threshold of a great department store." Within his model women and the department stores were seen in a symbiotic relationship in which the shops filled an elemental need for women. They didn't need to buy anything, thought Dubuisson, but they needed the atmosphere and the sight of "all those beautiful things." By this time the diagnosis of kleptomania was based on the assumption that it was irrational to steal things one did not need. Forensic specialists concluded that people who did so were not legally responsible for their acts. Supporting this was a body of psychiatric literature agreeing with the concept of legal irresponsibility of the kleptomaniac in the commission of a crime. It all had a determining impact on the judicial treatment of bourgeois women caught shoplifting; nearly all such women caught shoplifting were acquitted by the French courts. Typical in emphasizing wealth as a critical factor in assigning the diagnosis was Dubuisson who found most of the women he examined to be well-to-do and even rich. That led him to generalize about the women he examined that "if they were women who had money and who still stole, one could conclude that they were suffering from a *debilite mentale*." By this means, shoplifting came to be connected with weakness of spirit and low intelligence in women.[49]

When Patricia O'Brien looked at over 200 case studies of shoplifting in late nineteenth century France she found that most of the diagnosed kleptomaniacs were not guilty of isolated thefts but seemed to have stolen over a considerable period of time. Those case studies caused O'Brien to declare that "the examining specialist was more than just a filter through whom the patient's testimony passed. One is struck by the degree to which he created the diagnosis by reconstructing the past life of the patient. Personal history came to determine the meaning of the present behavior of the accused individual. The theft itself was nearly obscured by the psychiatrist's concern with pathology — those diseased events that preceded, resulted in, and survived the act of theft and were woven together from the fabric of a pathological condition." Sexuality and heredity were investigated with particular care. Specialists in medicine looked for "sexual physiological accidents" such as pregnancy, menopause, and menstruation that led to the "auto-toxic" condition. In one study of 104 department store thieves (all female) 35 were menstruating, ten were menopausal and five were pregnant. Thus, almost half of the accused women were considered to be in a weakened and monomaniacally susceptible state. Therefore, deviant behavior could be traced to physiological origins—"women were diseased by their sexuality. As a result, all women, even the most honest, were, at various periods in their lives—'genital stages'—susceptible to criminal behavior," concluded O'Brien. Allegedly, the most dangerous stage of all was menopause. Females stole because they were having problems of a pathological nature with their reproductive organs.[50]

Besides the physiological approach, O'Brien found in the case studies the less widely held opinion that females sought sexual gratification through theft as orgasmic reactions were frequently recorded in the clinical case studies. As one accused woman said, she got more pleasure from her thefts than from "the father of her children." Psychiatrists regularly appeared to have found what they were looking for. Considered to be prime candidates for the designation of kleptomaniac were women with regular or difficult pregnancies, irregular cycles, menopause, nervous conditions, dead husbands, bad marriages, poor health, and suicidal tendencies. Even in cases where no sickness was obvious, the examining officials were capable of locating a problem. One young woman in excellent health with regular cycles, and with no hereditary pathology, was nonetheless classified as a kleptomaniac. Psychiatrists decided that a minor, long-forgotten vision and hearing problem experienced years earlier following her marriage was the problem. Although a few men were diagnosed as kleptomaniacs, O'Brien noted that "on the whole, then, what were called women's sicknesses, hysteria, and hereditary weaknesses became the essential elements in the etiology of kleptomania. The examining specialist clearly sought these out when he encountered a woman of the bourgeoisie charged with theft." By the end of the nineteenth century there was a general agreement that victims of kleptomania stole because of a loss of reason, either temporary or hereditary, and were motivated by physiological malfunction, sexual frustration, or both. It was an era in which the concept of the "weaker sex" was prominent. Women were considered less intelligent, more emotional, and more susceptible to mental illness and violent outbursts. Kleptomania studies were just another proof of the inferiority of females.[51]

Along with the consumer revolution at the end of the nineteenth century was a critique of consumption to which the diagnosis of kleptomania made a contribution. The rise of the "irresistible cult of consumption" involved ethical and moral issues in an increasing literature of social criticism which featured kleptomania as being only a more deviant form of the need to consume. A small number of medical experts began to put the blame on department stores arguing that easily accessible goods were temptations "better than Satan himself could devise," placed in the path of weak and impressionable creatures. Large retailers created artificial needs for goods by seducing their customers with clever advertising and marketing. New opportunities were created for handling goods which were not possible in smaller outlets. Those large stores provided greater freedom to customers to pocket the goods. A characteristic of the new culture of consumption was not the purchase or use of goods— it was the possession of them.[52]

Emile Zola wrote, "Then there were the women with a mania for stealing, a perversion of desire, a new kind of neurosis that was classified by a mental specialist who had observed the acute result of the temptation exercised on them by the department stores."[53]

Back in the United States, kleptomania as a form of middle-class shoplifting did not begin to become an issue until the late 1870s. For example, there was no discussion of kleptomania in the uproar that followed the arrest of Elizabeth B. Phelps in December 1870 on a charge of stealing a small package of candy in the R. H. Macy and Co. department store. She was a socially prominent New York feminist, and her case drew a lot of media attention. The idea that Phelps could be accused of so tawdry a crime was inconceivable. A large group of letter-writing citizens, along with various newspaper editors, were unanimous in condemning Macy employees for apprehending her and the police for charging her. Not entertained at all by the public was the possibility that Phelps was guilty. The single issue involved was class.[54]

But in 1887 Dr. Orpheus Everts, superintendent of the Cincinnati Sanitarium argued that kleptomania was a valid form of mental illness which existed, but only in a dependent relationship to other symptoms. With regard to kleptomania he argued that a "natural desire to accumulate exaggerated by disease" comprised the reality of kleptomania. He felt this combination of disease and desire to be a valid mental disorder. Everts illustrated his thesis with the case of a 39-year-old widow with children who was admitted to his asylum as an hysteric with a history of shoplifting. This woman was diagnosed as suffering from "womb disease mania" which the doctor described as "larceny and eroticism with hysteria." Such explanatory models also reinforced the established notions about class and gender. They defined the reproductive functions of females as inherently diseased. If manias could be traced to the womb, as models such as the one Everts put forward implied, then the sexuality of women could be associated with behavioral irregularities and sickness. As it became a medically and socially credible diagnosis kleptomania reinforced beliefs about female weakness.[55]

Late in 1896, wealthy American Ella Castle was arrested on shoplifting charges in London, England. She pled guilty on seven counts but was immediately released as not responsible for her behavior because she was a kleptomaniac. It was a case which received much publicity in America. One of a trio of specialists who examined Ella, Dr. Grigg, testified at the trial: "She is intensely neurotic. The condition of things—a disease of the upper portion of the uterus—is a very common accompaniment of various forms of mania in women, such as melancholia, religious mania, nymphomania, and I have seen it in several cases of kleptomania. It is invariably coupled with much mental disturbance. The condition I discovered is quite sufficient to account for any form of mental vagaries which are as well known to affect a certain class of women (neurotic) with disordered menstruation. Her bowel condition would aggravate this." Once back in the United States Ella consulted doctors at the Philadelphia Polyclinic Hospital where she was treated by a team of physicians. In charge of her treatment was Dr. Solomon Solis-Cohen who identified her medical symptoms as disordered menstruation, uterine irregularities, and hemorrhoids. From physical problems such as these, the doctor reported, "various forms of mania in women" commonly appear, including kleptomania. At her trail Ella appeared with all the props that bourgeois women had by then learned helped their cause. Castle wore concealing black veils, appeared with smelling salts and uniformed medical attendants, and had a number of fainting spells. She exhibited every symptom a respectable kleptomaniac was expected to manifest: menstrual problems, loss of memory, frequent nervous episodes, and pains in the head. Additionally, she was married to a wealthy man said to be "very generous" to his wife and completely ignorant of his spouse's stealing.[56]

Faced with the unnerving reality of respectable females stealing items from stores, physicians explained kleptomania in terms of sexuality and feminine weakness. Attempting to understand what was deemed irrational behavior, the general public and doctors accepted a view of women that limited them to a biological dependency, to behavior controlled by emotions and to prescribed social roles. It came together in the close association of medical "fact" and popular ideology. In the earliest, French interpretation, kleptomania was described as the impulse of a diseased imagination and marked by the absence of economic need. That view was accepted widely in both Europe and the United States as the impairment of the individual's voluntary powers. Not explicitly gender specific in the beginning, on both sides of the Atlantic the diagnosis was quickly associated almost exclusively with women, specifically with the female reproductive economy, considered to be the seat of the disorder. Most shoplifters were women but the association of shopping activities with biological processes was a leap that was securely rooted in the Victorian period intellectual assumptions. Closely involved was the nineteenth century medical and moral debate about the relation of insanity to the female reproductive system.[57]

Menstrual disorders, especially, were integral to medical explanations of seemingly motiveless stealing. What physicians called "ovarian insanity" was transformed into the more specific label of kleptomania. Uterine disease became a diagnostic catch-all. Labeling someone a kleptomaniac removed responsibility from the afflicted woman and made any moral judgment of her behavior inappropriate. If a kleptomaniac was under the control of biology, concluded doctors, the kleptomaniac was physically defective, but not evil. Physicians labeled Castle a kleptomaniac because they felt she had lost the power of reason; she suffered from hysteria triggered by specific physiological malfunction. It all meshed in the many popular prejudices and assumptions that "sexuality was the root of female behavior." Medical opinion, coupled with popular notions of female character, allowed and encouraged theoretically impartial courts to change a criminal act into a physical symptom. Dr. Arthur Conan Doyle expressed the main elements of the case in a letter to the *London Times* urging the newspaper to intervene on behalf of Castle: "If there is any doubt of moral responsibility the benefit of the doubt should certainly be given to one whose sex and position … give her a double claim to our consideration: It is the consulting room and not to the cell that she should be sent." Illustrated by the letter were the coupled cultural assumptions about middle-class women and about female sexuality.[58]

As researcher Elaine Abelson said of kleptomania; "Only middle-class women seemed to suffer from it; stealing by members of other classes was simple theft." Doctors and lawyers in the late 1880s in America defended respectable, middle-class females accused of shoplifting by saying little more than "she is a respectable well-connected lady, but evidently a kleptomaniac." Most of the time it worked; mostly those women were acquitted. Instability was believed to be rooted in women's nature and that made it easy to see why kleptomania found such ready acceptance. The label

served as both excuse and explanation. If shoplifting had not been interpreted as an illness it would have to have been understood as a crime. The
possibility that respectable, middle-class women could "sink into such a
moral cesspool and forfeit the esteem and love of their best friends for a
bottle of cosmetic" was unthinkable.[59]

The labeling of shoplifters as kleptomaniacs reached its peak toward
the end of the 1800s and largely disappeared by 1920. However, it would
still rate a media mention now and again, right up to the present time.
For example, when the *New York Times* published a general article on
shoplifting in Connecticut in December 1998, it declared there were five
general types of shoplifters, one of which was the "kleptomaniac."[60]

Yet those who dealt with the problem around the turn of the century
continued to be totally skeptical. When store detective Amelia de Santis
was asked in 1913 about her experiences with the issue, she remarked,
"Kleptomania? Fudge! That is only a term that is applied to a thief who
happens to have social standing."[61]

One of the reasons the diagnosis faded away was that the class-biased
filter was usually applied earlier in the process. That is, retailers released
such women without laying charges. As well, sentences for shoplifting
eased from their former draconian dimensions. It became less and less necessary to save women of the upper classes from the system by the use of
the label. Labeling women as kleptomaniacs also served a useful and more
general purpose in that it reinforced the idea that women were inferior,
overly erratic, too emotional, etc. With time, this kind of labeling became
less politically and socially acceptable.

When the women excused from shoplifting charges were wealthy or
well-to-do, what was almost never mentioned at the time was that many
of these women had little or no money to use with their own discretion.
They were wealthy by virtue of the status, position, and occupation of
their husbands or fathers. Often the money they had on them at the time
of their arrest was all specifically earmarked for certain purchases, with
the husband expecting a full accounting of every penny spent. Thus the
wealthy woman was often in the same position in a department store as
her status-poorer sisters; both wanted something and neither had the
money to spend. One of the few mentions of this idea came in an article
in 1915 written by an unnamed superintendent of a large department store.
He noted his company took steps against shoplifters because it was eating
into profits so much and "it was beginning to demoralize the sales force
… as they came to know that women of social prestige and good name
were constantly escaping penalties justly due them." That was when the
upper classes were simply released from the store without prosecution.

Word went out that the store would make active prosecution in all cases "whatever the antecedents or connections of the persons involved, seeking full penalties from the courts for the offenses committed." The superintendent then detailed three cases of wealthy women from rich families and with rich husbands but no access to any of the money, except under rigorous oversight from the husbands. The same was said to be true for workingmen, who had less, but also allowed females little access to it. He said that "it would help to share that little and relieve the absolute financial dependence of these girls, many of whom had been themselves wage-earners before the marriages." In conclusion he wrote; "all too often the woman shoplifter was the product of conditions imposed by the husband … let us not forget the culpability of the man who humbles his wife by excluding her from that which is justly hers— either a competency of her own or a joint proprietorship in the family income."[62]

Just how much was being lost to shoplifters in this early period was unknown. One New York City merchant was quoted in 1872 as saying "I make an allowance of about two percent for such losses." Eleven years later another retailer made a similar assessment, although most had no idea at all. Surviving R. H. Macy & Company bookkeeping records from 1875–1876 showed "shorts" of from 2.5 percent to five percent. Even in those years the customers were thought to be the major reason for such shorts.[63]

In more recent times retailers had a good idea as to their losses due to "shrinkage"— the industry term. They start with the opening inventory, add in the purchases from suppliers and subtract the sales to customers. The closing figure represents the number of items which should be on the shelves or in the stockroom. When the physical inventory comes up short of that the difference is the shrinkage, often thought to be wholly due to shoplifters, and often attributed completely to shoplifters by the media. However, a second major cause of shrinkage is from employee theft. A third is from things such as supplier problems whereby a wholesaler "accidentally" packs cartons of widgets with 99 items instead of the 100 listed on the carton. Math errors also play a part with clerks ringing up wrong prices. Since record keeping does not keep track of the number of widgets but rather their dollar value, error can creep in from procedures such as selling items at marked-down prices, but not accurately adjusting the records. As a percentage of shrinkage, shoplifting may be responsible for only one-third or less of the total.

By the time of World War I, shoplifting had become firmly established as an urban problem centered in the large department stores, but not limited to them. It was a large enough problem that retailers had turned to hiring employees—store detectives—whose sole function was to deal with this issue and other security matters. Shoplifting came to be seen as a crime committed almost exclusively by women. Apprehended females from the lower classes were mostly prosecuted. They were regarded and treated as criminals, often drawing harsh penalties for the activity. Apprehended females from the upper classes were mostly not prosecuted. When they were, they were usually regarded and treated as being ill, labeled kleptomaniacs and released.

- *Chapter 2* •

SHOPLIFTING IS PICKING UP, 1919–1946

"[Women] follow the large sales and they steal."—William Murphy, store detective, 1920

"Sometimes rather than risk a lawsuit or lose the business of a shoplifter's wealthy friends, we let her walk out with the loot."—Store manager, 1945

In the aftermath of World War I, the number of shoplifters shot up dramatically. Sentences tended to be more lenient, although repeat offenders were still often harshly treated. On one day in May 1920, 17 females were arraigned in New York on charges of shoplifting, involving separate incidents. Twelve of them were first offenders, all of whom were released on suspended sentences or freed upon the payment of a fine. One of the others was sentenced to six months in jail while another was incarcerated for two years.[1]

Just two weeks later 52 people were arraigned on shoplifting charges. Most of them were women, "as usual," although the exact number was not stated. All of the 52 had been arrested by agents of the Stores' Mutual Protective Association (SMPA). A representative of the District Attorney's office reported that his investigation of this type of crime "had shown a large increase in shoplifting since the advances in prices." This was a reference to post-war inflation. Yet one month later a reporter with the *New York Times* stated that despite the record number of arraignments for shoplifting "it has been noted that not in a single case has the high cost of living been pleaded as an excuse for stealing."[2]

Later in June 1920, a total of 20 people were arraigned in one day. Most of the women were released upon the payment of fines. Three men were involved, all second offenders, and all received jail time. William Jaspar got three months in the workhouse for taking one pair of gloves; Louis

29

Nathan was sentenced to six months to three years for stealing six pairs
of socks; Samuel Ringler received 30 days in the workhouse for shoplifting one suit of clothes. From June 1 to June 19, fines totaling $4,000 were
received in the Court of Special Sessions from shoplifters. So troublesome
were the numbers that shoplifters were warned by the justices in Special
Sessions that more frequent and severe prison sentences would be given
in the future to discourage the increasing number of thefts in department
stores.[3]

Not that it had much effect. On July 1, 1920, 42 people were arraigned
for shoplifting, all of them women. All had been arrested by store detectives with the SMPA. Most of those arraigned were young females; 20 pled
guilty. All but one were released on probation after paying a fine of $25
to $75 to the Court of Special Sessions. Inez Chase was sentenced to four
months in the workhouse for stealing a handbag worth $26.75.[4]

A couple of months later 14 women were arraigned on one day. Eight
were fined while the other six received jail time at the workhouse. Three
received 30 day sentences, one got 15 days, the other two received one day
each.[5]

In the summer of 1920 the problem was so severe that the large stores
in New York, cooperating through the SMPA, began a campaign to clear
their stores of amateur shoplifting. They were satisfied that they had already
reduced the presence of professional shoplifters in their establishments to
a minimum. That move to suppress the amateurs came because store detectives had, said a report, "found that while they had practically driven the
professional thief into other fields the amount of stealing did not dimin-
ish to the extent expected. The amateurs had overrun the stores and were
pilfering without the discrimination of the professional." During the first
six months of 1920 it was estimated that 3,600 people, mostly females,
were apprehended in SMPA-affiliated stores for shoplifting. Not all of
them were arrested, "for some were allowed to pay for the goods found
upon them and others, because of certain circumstances connected with
the cases, were warned and allowed to go." Of the 3,600 people, 90 percent were women. Just 10 percent of the total number were described as
professional shoplifters.[6]

A main function of the SMPA remained that of acting as a clearing-
house. When an arrest was made in one store, all the other affiliated members were notified of the details. Said William Murphy, chief detective for
the SMPA, "There come to our net women of all ages and descriptions,
and of varied degrees of intelligence; married and single, with and without families. They follow the large sales and they steal." As to their behavior after being detected Murphy remarked, "These amateurs when caught

become incoherent and this gives way to hysteria when it appears they are going to be arrested. In court their defense is nearly always the same. They bring forward character witnesses and they are ever the devoted wife or the loving mother and their offense was not a conscious error — they merely slipped from the path of righteousness."[7]

Nearing Christmas of 1921, with the annual rush of shoplifters well underway, W. Trenholm, secretary of the SMPA, declared the activity was down that year, compared to previous years at the same time. "The reason shoplifting has decreased is jail sentences from judges," declared Trenholm. As was the usual case in the Christmas season, the SMPA had reinforced its staff for the holidays. As well, special details of men from police headquarters were present in the stores and on the sidewalks of the shopping districts.[8]

Yet on a January day in 1922, the Court of Special Sessions disposed of 75 shoplifting cases while on the following day it dealt with 55 cases. On that latter day 51 of the accused were women. The men and most of the women accused were first offenders. All of those were released on payment of fines of $25. When one woman was unable to give any reason for taking a raincoat, Justice McInerney observed: "Of all the persons who have been arraigned as shoplifters I have not seen one who could give a satisfactory explanation why they committed these crimes." Among the group of 55 were five women with babies in their arms. One of those, Marie Parfrey was sentenced to 10 days in the workhouse for the theft of $49 worth of goods from Gimbel Brothers.[9]

Commenting on the type of person shoplifting, an unnamed store detective said, "It is not the people from the lower east side or similar neighborhoods we have to watch ... but the stenographer, the nurse, the clerk and the rich woman. These are the people who today pick up everything from a lip stick to a $200 dress and walk off with it." A new method in the arsenal of shoplifting tricks was the third hand. An artificial hand was placed where the real hand was expected to be. Then the real hand worked through a front opening in the coat, stowing items in a big inside pocket. Declaring that a harsher approach was in effect, the detective said that leniency extended toward "well-sponsored" thieves was no longer extended. At his store they were apprehending fewer but arresting more. In his store in 1921, 619 people were apprehended for shoplifting; almost 400 of them were arrested. "If it is a first offense and the girl is young, has a good job and her record is clear, she is not arrested. But if several articles are found on her and there is a suspicious slant to the case, she is arrested and the matter settled in court. The newspapers can do a great deal by giving wide publicity to shoplifting cases. The weekly publishing of offenders' names as some of the papers are doing at present is one of the best ways of lessening this evil." While he said store detectives made allowances for youth and for thoughtlessness, such was not the case for kleptomania. "We detectives don't believe there is such an animal."[10]

With regard to the type of people brought before him as accused shoplifters, an unnamed judge of New York's Court of Special Sessions said: "The majority of these girls are from 17 to 25 … and the majority of the thefts were articles of adornment, perfume, small plunder. In many cases there is no reason for these girls stealing. They have good jobs. Have all the money they need. It isn't the woman or man who is hungry, who is down and out, today, who is doing the petty thieving. Occasionally we get drug addicts among older shoplifters, and when a man is caught shoplifting he is pretty apt to be a drug fiend." He added that "offenders for less than $50 we let off with a fine. The professional who has a bad record gets three years or more. This type is pretty well cleared out of New York now." In conclusion he remarked, "It is the be-rouged and be-furred young things that crowd the court calender now. The girl with a good home and a good job. The girl who does not need money or food. Her one vice is vanity, and vanity leads her to do strange things. It is a phase of modern life which is assuming serious proportions."[11]

On a March day in 1922, 11 women were called into Women's Court before Magistrate Silberman. All were first offenders charged with shoplifting. They ranged in age from 17 to 23 and appeared in fur coats. All were bound over for the Court of Special Sessions. A reporter at the scene noted that "the whole courtroom, including the Magistrate, the attendants, policemen and witnesses in other cases, stared in amazement at the gorgeous collection of prisoners. Brilliant plumage nodded rhythmically as several buried their faces in handkerchiefs, plain and lace-edged." Silberman told the 11 that "not one-half of 1 percent of the women he had seen wearing sealskins in Fifth Ave were rightfully entitled to wear them." It was a reference to a walk he had taken on that street a couple of days earlier during which he saw among the throng of shoppers many women who had appeared before him in the previous six months. He thought it was evidence that the seemingly "unquenchable desire" to dress as well as wealthier women caused these women to take a chance to obtain some of the finery they longed for. Twenty-five years earlier a woman who appeared in public wearing a sealskin coat was considered to be the wife or daughter of a millionaire, but today, Silberman asserted, "the girl who earns but $10 to $15 weekly wears the same coat and is generally attired as well as the girl or woman in much better station financially." He felt it was that desire to dress as well as the rich and "that continuous sex flaunting in the public press of accounts of some ball or dance or other function, detailing what this or that woman wore, which have inculcated in these girls the desire to imitate those in better finances."[12]

By 1924 the war metaphor was in use. A reporter wrote: "Waging war upon shoplifters is almost as much a part of the efficient conduct of a department store as the delivery of packages. These meccas of merchandise are the happy hunting grounds for a legion of men and women intent upon getting something for nothing. There are no truces in the conflict between the stores and their despoilers. The struggle is especially bitter during November and December, although there are many who do their Christmas stealing early." William Murphy, still chief detective for the SMPA, estimated that just five percent of shoplifters were professionals. Previous to his SMPA employment, Murphy was a detective sergeant for the New York Police Department (NYPD) for 16 years.[13]

Among the more popular methods favored by shoplifters was the box with a false bottom. Another involved the use of a huge pocket inside the front of the skirt with an elastic waistband which enabled the thief to drop such large articles as three or four men's shirts or a bolt of silk into the pocket. It was not sewed on the bottom edge but tied by a string with one end in easy reach of the shopper. Thus, with one tug she could open the pocket, causing the items to fall to the floor. This was an emergency measure used if apprehension seemed imminent. Among the more popular items for amateurs to shoplift were, according to Murphy, silk hosiery, then necklaces of all kinds, silk underwear third, and gloves fourth. Murphy commented, "During the war there was something in the general nature of things which seemed to render women more daring. Women of good family, who had never done a dishonest act before in their lives, went in for the milder forms of shoplifting." When the wartime prosperity ended and business reconstruction set in, shoplifting increased somewhat, he thought. The reason for that, felt Murphy, "may have been in the sustained desire of women for beautiful things, despite the fact that the end of the war brought with it the end of the period of inflated wages."[14]

In a 1925 interview with a store detective who worked for a large department store, the unnamed man estimated that 95 percent of shoplifting was done by women, with only 10 percent committed by people in need. He also estimated that 65 percent of the stealing from stores in New York was done by women who could readily afford to buy what they took; 10 percent was taken by those who had to steal or go without; with the remaining 25 percent stolen by professionals. Most shoplifting was done on Saturdays, he said. It was known in one store as "stenographer's day" as it was then that silk hosiery and underwear, handkerchiefs, necklaces and the like were most likely to disappear. Frequently about half the arrests made in his store took place on Saturdays. Over the course of a year those arrests in his store totaled 800 to 1,000. Monday was the next biggest day for shoplifting. One prominent New York store then had a protective staff of 60 people: 26 uniformed men, 10 plainclothesmen, and 24 women in plainclothes. Most of the women were former salesclerks.[15]

Some minor attention was paid to other causes of shrinkage. A 1924 article by a woman working as a store detective in a large department store devoted about half its length to employee thefts and scams. But such articles were very rare.[16]

By 1927, another favorite shoplifter method was also in use. When Robert F. Murphy was arrested for shoplifting, officials discovered the scam whereby he returned to stores with the goods he had stolen to get cash refunds from clerks.[17]

George C. Henderson was another man employed as a store detective who worked in a large, unnamed department store. No store liked to have its name publicly associated with shoplifting, any facet of it. He guessed that 75 percent to 90 percent of the shoplifters were otherwise honest people who were unable to resist the temptation to secure a bit of jewelry or finery and who stole on the spur of the moment, without premeditation, because it seemed so easy: "They start stealing because it seems easy and they continue because greed breeds greed and the human love for possessions is insatiable." A circumstance he felt that made it difficult for regular city police to handle department store shoplifting cases successfully was the fact that many eminently wealthy and respectable women were caught stealing in the course of a year. He had never met a store detective who did not have on his "secret" files the names of some of the best families attached to confessions exacted, along with compensation, "as the price of exemption from prosecution. Several prominent men whom I know have a private arrangement by which their wives' thefts are charged up to them and the term larceny is glossed over by alienists certifying that it is not moral turpitude at all but a disease — kleptomania."[18]

Noting that department stores did not wish to call in the police to arrest someone who had stolen a pair of socks, it was also true that if stores tolerated such petty theft they would soon become bankrupt. From that dilemma evolved the house detective. Henderson elaborated: "When a department store operative arrests a person for stealing, the thief is taken to the search room where he is forced to sign a confession, pay for the stolen article and promise never again to return to the store, under penalty of immediate arrest and exposure." He added that: "Unless the larcenist is a known or suspected professional, he or she is not turned over to the police but is released on the first offense with a stern warning. Generally the fright and threats of disgrace serve to set the offender's feet on the right path."[19]

According to the NYPD, in 1924 there were 943 women and 221 men arrested on shoplifting charges. In 1929 the figures were, respectively, 1,184 and 239. Police claimed that shoplifting by professionals had been reduced to about two percent of 1929's total offences. Most of those arrested females were 17 to 23 years of age. As far as the NYPD was concerned, shoplifters seldom came from the poorer classes; usually they came from fairly good homes, that about two percent of those arrested were foreign born, that there was no perceptible correlation between shoplifting and unemployment, and "kleptomania is practically non-existent." Still showing confusion between shoplifting and employee theft this account quoted police officials as recommending as a preventive measure that "since a large percentage of 'jobs' are by employees, be careful in hiring."[20]

Getting tough on crime was not something new in the 1980s and 1990s. Back around 1930, New York State had the Baumes law on the books. This law resembled the more recent "three strikes and you're out" legislation, except that four strikes was the magic number. Shoplifting was prosecuted under larceny statutes. Petty larceny involved smaller amounts of goods and was only a misdemeanor. Shoplifting items worth more than a specific number of dollars led to a felony charge of grand larceny. The dollar amount cut-off varied over time. At the time the Baumes measure was debated, the police had hoped that all shoplifting would be brought under the Baumes law, not just the felony cases.[21]

One of the first people to fall victim to the Baumes statute was 29-year-old Ruth St. Clair, who was arrested in December 1929 for stealing a number of articles from a department store. When she was convicted early in 1930 she faced life in prison since it marked her a four-time felony offender under the Baumes crime-curbing act. In 1920 she pled guilty to stealing two dresses and got one year in jail. In 1924 she stole a coat from a department store, pled guilty, and was sentenced to six months in the workhouse. Finally, in 1926, she stole a coat from another department store, pled guilty, and got three years in prison. St. Clair's record compelled the judge to impose a life sentence, the first handed out to a woman since the law was enacted.[22]

The harshness of St. Clair's sentence led to much hullabaloo from the media, politicians, and so forth. However, the sentence was upheld by the United States Supreme Court, later in 1930. After spending eight years in prison St. Clair had her sentence commuted to time served and was released.[23]

At the start of the 1930s, store detectives were common in most retail establishments of any size in the New York area, varying in number from six in smaller shops to 100 in one very large department store. Still active was the SMPA, which was then passing around a "Rogues Gallery" of over 850 photos of people convicted as shoplifters, pickpockets, imposters or bad check passers. Imposters were considered just another type of shoplifter. Responsible for many store losses was the phrase "charge and take." Practically every store permitted its customers to take goods worth up to $10 if the customer signed her name and said she had an account.[24]

As president of the Girls' Service League, Maude Miner Hadden was familiar with the problem of shoplifting in the New York area in the early 1930s since her group had conducted studies of the issue. Agreeing that 95 percent of shoplifters before the Depression were women, she argued that the percentage had changed to 75 percent female since the onset of the Depression due to the greater numbers of men out of work. She thought the age range ran the gamut and that members of all economic classes were involved, "the rich because they do not wish to pay, the poor because they cannot. The latter are the greater number." At this time the SMPA was supported by 16 of the largest department stores as well as by some of the smaller ones. It kept complete records on all known shoplifters. Before the Depression, each year brought an average of 3,500 new names to the files; since then the number had been at the 4,000 mark, and sometimes beyond. Altogether the SMPA had over 55,000 names on record, amassed over its existence of some 15 years. Phones were manned by the organization all day. If Jane Doe was apprehended in Macy's trying to steal something, Macy's would phone to see if she was on file. Remarked Hadden, "If nothing is found in the files it may mean her release after a written confession of guilt and promise of reform; if, however, she has a record of previous thefts, no matter where, it usually means arrest." Her name went on a permanent record both in the store where the theft took place and at the SMPA.[25]

One study by the Girls' Service League involved 100 cases in a city prison. Seventy-one were between the ages of 18 and 30. Of the 100 women 16 were unemployed, 29 made less than $20 a week, 16 were in the $20 to $35 class, 32 were supported by families or husbands. No information was available on the rest. With regard to occupations, 23 were factory workers, 22 were houseworkers, maids or waitresses. The rest were clerks, saleswomen, milliners, etc. Most of the thefts were petty with only 10 involving as much as $50. The rest ranged from $1.50 to $40, with the greatest number, 24, in the $5 group. Taken by months, March and April had 32 arrests while October, November, and December had a total of 45 arrests. Said

Hadden, "Inasmuch as a department store is designed primarily to meet the purchasing needs of women, it is logical that they should form the great bulk of shoplifters." In a different study of 215 cases brought to trial for shoplifting during the Christmas season, it was found that 80 received sentences of a $25 fine or five days in prison, 36 had sentences suspended, 32 were put on probation, 30 received a $50 fine or 10 days, 22 were sent to the workhouse, five were sent to the penitentiary, five got a $100 fine or 30 days, two were transferred to the Children's Court, one was committed to the Hospital for the Insane, one received a $150 fine or 60 days, and one had the case dismissed. Of those 215 people, 206 had no previous court record. The conviction rate was extraordinarily high because stores did not proceed unless they were absolutely certain. One reason stemmed from a fear of lawsuits brought by anyone who was wrongly arrested.[26]

The first confessional article seems to have appeared in the July 1937 issue of *Atlantic*. Titled "A Kleptomaniac's Mind," this article related the anonymous author's long, personal story as a working, well-paid teacher who stole out of compulsion. Short on insight, the article was of the "poor me" type. Arrested once and taken to the store's office, the teacher remarked about the paper she signed: "The card says that you voluntarily acknowledge the theft of the articles listed, having received no promise of immunity." This woman then wrote "a compact with God" and gave up shoplifting. While such store forms used the word "voluntarily," it was misleading because the person involved often felt compelled to sign it to avoid the threatened police and court action from not signing.[27]

At the very end of the 1930s, shoplifting had become such a problem at the nation's largest retailer of women's clothing, S. Klein's on Union Square in New York City, that the retailer posted signs in five languages warning against it—English, Spanish, Italian, Polish, and Yiddish. Backing up that warning were 25 employees, called spotters, who averaged three or four arrests a day in total. Nevertheless, shoplifting cost Klein's $100,000 yearly. At Macy's the shoplifting toll was said to be $1 million annually. But that included losses to thefts by employees and the salaries of about 100 spotters. At Klein's the signing of a document was similar to that used by other retailers in that the signer agreed she really stole the merchandise, agreed to pay for it, promised never to darken the store again, and acknowledged awareness that if she was caught a second time she would be prosecuted for both the first and second offenses. Klein's then had glass-enclosed booths— called "crying rooms"—where offenders were parked for several hours before undergoing a "trial." While this account in *Forum* admitted that "store employees do their share of shoplifting," it also pointed out that the SMPA "ostensibly is engaged only in suppressing shoplifting by the public."[28]

With the coming of World War II, little was written about shoplifters until near the end of the conflict. However, they had been busy. A female store detective in Canada stated that in the few years since the outbreak of war, shoplifting had almost doubled. One of the reasons she thought responsible was that "during such times there is always a lowering of ethical standards." Other causes she put forward were the higher costs of living, an increase in self-service stores and less retail staff because of war shortages. "The minute food was rationed the theft curve began to mount. The strange thing is that as rationing is being gradually reduced, there is no diminution in this form of petty thefts. There seems to be a peculiar fascination about shoplifting which creates addicts. Once people have formed the habit and learned the tricks, they appear incapable of resisting the temptation of securing something for nothing."[29]

By that time, 1944, many stores exhibited a sign at the cashier's desk declaring that handbags and parcels were "subject to examination," and asking for the cooperation of patrons. However, readers of the article were presumably calmed by a further explanation that the warning could not be enforced and that no cashier had the authority to insist on inspection. As long as a customer was in the store, no theft had been committed. Women shoplifters remained far more numerous than men, and this female store detective again confirmed the reason: "because there are more women shoppers." Going further into the reason for shoplifting, she said that too many husbands believed assertions that the cost of living had not gone up, so they allowed their wives too little housekeeping money and the women had to resort to theft to keep the men fed the way they wanted. Admitting there was no doubt some of the women were poor managers, or lost money gambling, or spent money extravagantly on themselves, the detective added that a good many of those women confided in her and she was certain that much of the trouble could be traced to short allowances. "At the same time, I must admit that there is little shoplifting in the poorer districts. It is seen at its worst in middle-class well-to-do neighborhoods. The majority of shoplifters don't need to steal. They do it for fun or pure devilment — I'm not sure which," she concluded. Her last statement implied that, of course, the cost of living was not involved.[30]

When a Canadian store manager was asked in 1945 if a shoplifter had learned her lesson if she was released from the store without being charged he replied: "Maybe she has. But most of them don't. It gets in their blood." Asked why his store didn't have them arrested, he said: "Sometimes we do. But not often. It's too dangerous. Some people actually hope we will call the police. Then, unless we can make our charge stick, they can sue us!" When the reporter asked if the store always apprehended shoplifters it observed, the manager commented: "Not always. We try to take the long-range view. Sometimes rather than risk a lawsuit or lose the business of a shoplifter's wealthy friends, we let her walk out with the loot. But never, of course, if her tastes are too expensive. We might overlook the theft of a scarf or pair of gloves but not that of a fur coat or expensive jewelry." Sometimes when a shoplifter walked out with items, the store phoned the woman's husband and told him his wife bought a fur hat but neglected to pay for it and would he be so kind as to mail the store a cheque. Usually he did. At this store about 20 percent of those apprehended pled absent-mindedness.[31]

Managers at large outlets in the area argued there was little shoplifting in the poorer neighborhoods. Most offenders were from middle-class districts. Some merchants guessed that between 3 percent and 11 percent of their customers would shoplift if given the chance. All those store managers, and their detectives, had only scorn for the kleptomania label. As one manager said, "If you live on the wrong side of the tracks they call it theft. If you own a lorgnette and live on Snob Hill it's kleptomania." Remarked a store detective, "all of them act deliberately and with premeditation. Kleptomania is only a corny excuse they resort to when caught." Reportedly a merchant doing $50,000 worth of business in a year usually set his shoplifting losses at between $200 and $450 a year, or from 0.4 percent to 0.9 percent.[32]

In London, England, in 1946 reporter Peter Duffield was moved to write, "Woman might take a sharp glance at herself today and reflect that despite her immortalized purity she stands unchallenged as the world's No. 1 potential and actual thief, pilferer and stealer of articles from shops." He added that "the act of shoplifting ... is today a country-wide menace, from which the long, light fingers of Woman are responsible nearly one hundred per cent." No one knew how much was lost to shoplifting but London's Metropolitan Police, who logged 1,477 cases in their area in 1936, reported an all-time peak of 2,431 in 1942. London then had about 100 store detectives employed by the larger retailers. Eighty percent of them were female, "often under the supervision of a male chief." One such was Lucy Marmon (a nom de plume) who said, "I keep my eye mainly on women's hands." Four factors were cited as responsible for increased wartime shoplifting: shortage of goods, scant coupon allowance, shortage of watchful shop assistants, lack of wrapping paper. Said one detective, formerly with Scotland Yard, "I don't believe all these claims for kleptomania. In some instances, there are people who are genuinely in need, but the majority of our cases are women who are just too mean to pay."[33]

During this period between the two World Wars the concept of kleptomania was little used or discussed, one of the reasons being that most of the "respectable" women either were not apprehended, or were apprehended and released. Thus there was less need to use it. When the concept was raised, it continued to draw scorn and derision from those in retailing. Shoplifters continued to be seen as mostly middle-class (or higher class) females. The youngest ages reported for offenders were 17 to 18 years old. They were regarded as adults, albeit young ones. If younger people were involved in shoplifting, it must have been to such a small extent that it did not bother retailers, or it went unmentioned. Stores themselves displayed their own ambivalence by regularly not charging those they apprehended, including some not from the favored classes. This was due to a fear of lawsuits and just general bad publicity that might accumulate for a store with a reputation for zealously prosecuting offenders. Women still did the bulk of the shopping and undoubtedly were a majority of offenders. However, since the belief that shoplifters were always female likely led to store detectives devoting all their attention to observing women, it could easily have become a self-fulfilling prophecy. Store losses continued to be wholly attributed to shoplifters, although no one had any real idea how much those losses might be. Any idea that retailers might contribute to their losses through the open display of goods, a lack of sufficient staff to monitor customers, or an ambivalent prosecution policy was also little mentioned or discussed, either in the general media or the trade publications.

Chapter 3

TELEVISION REACHES STORES AND WATCHES YOU, 1947–1959

"It's nearly always a woman.... Amateur or professional, beauty or battle-ax, she usually gets caught."—*Saturday Evening Post*, 1949

"Most foodlifters start out modestly by stealing something small— usually a quarter pound of butter."— Store detective, 1952

In the 15 years following World War II, a smattering of attention was devoted by academics to the psychological study of shoplifting. One of the few efforts made was a 1947 study by Northwestern University psychiatrist Dr. Alex Arieff who studied 338 shoplifting cases referred to Chicago's Municipal Psychiatric Institute between 1941 and 1946. He found many of those people to be "of social and political consequence and high intelligence." Of those 338 patients observed, he declared 77 percent had some definite mental, emotional or physical disorder. For a large percentage the diagnosis was "acute anxiety state with mental depression." Arieff stated there were four classes of shoplifters: 1) professionals, who were usually considered mentally normal and tried in Criminal Court; 2) general delinquents for whom shoplifting was part of a defective personality; 3) kleptomaniacs, or compulsive shoplifters; 4) normal individuals who stole on impulse while emotionally disturbed. In that group of 338 were 313 women and 25 men. The largest age groups were the 17 to 20 year olds, for whom "desire far outstrips buying power," and the 36 to 50 age group, "chiefly women, a period of increased tension" caused, in many cases, "by the onset and development of the menopause."

When he gave intelligence tests to a subgroup of the 338, Arieff concluded that 87 had normal intelligence, 14 were borderline, and 2 were feeble-minded. Fifty-seven percent of the 338 had no previous arrests. Of those with previous arrests, 24 percent were apprehended for the same offense—which meant 145 of the group had priors, 35 of them for shoplifting.

To dispose of his cases, Arieff returned 49 percent of them to court for supervision; recommended psychiatric treatment with court supervision for 36 percent, and turned over 5 percent for correctional care in institutions.[1]

Profiling one of the nation's biggest and busiest department stores in a *Saturday Evening Post* article late in 1949, the journalist used the subhead: "It's nearly always a woman. Each year she steals $75,000,000 in goods from store counters. Amateur or professional, beauty or battle-ax, she usually gets caught." The last part was certainly not true. Reporter Stewart Sterling called it a hidden tax the public paid without thinking much about it — a sum equal to about one percent of the country's annual department store sales total. To that, Sterling added another $25 million or so for theft prevention. Confusion still existed on whether a store could apprehend a suspect for shoplifting inside the store, or whether employees had to wait for the suspect to pass through the exit. Sterling declared that "local ground rules vary somewhat in different cities, but, in general, if a thief carries a stolen article 200 feet from the counter at which it was on display, it is considered sufficient evidence to hold up in court." An average shoplifter's take reportedly was less than $15 worth of goods, with about 100,000 individual thefts each week. Those were supposedly the ones who got away with it. The total of shoplifting attempts was said to be around one million per month. Nineteen out of every 20 shoplifters were women; 8 of each 20 were between the ages 18 and 23 with another 8 of 20 being 38 to 45 years old. Sterling reported that kleptomaniacs amounted to less than one in a hundred. A store detective supplied that figure but acknowledged he had plenty of trouble with larcenous-minded women who, when apprehended, "tried to put over the idea they suffered from an overpowering compulsion to take things that didn't belong to them." According to Sterling, 80 percent of the $250,000 daily take was lifted by professional thieves. He added that more than half of all the professionals were narcotic addicts. Protection staff in department stores numbered roughly one for every 100 employees. In this particular store, only protection staff were allowed to make apprehensions. Other store employees could only point out a suspected shoplifting to a security person. In this large store, there was no instance on record of any customer ever reporting a theft by a shoplifter to the store.[2]

A store detective who worked for a large supermarket chain based in Chicago reported that in their 150 Chicago stores, the company apprehended 698 foodlifters in 1951. Only one was a kleptomaniac, only two were hardship cases — mothers with children and absolutely no money — with the other 695 being plain, ordinary customers, mainly housewives, who couldn't pass up a chance to take something for nothing. Invariably they had enough money to pay for the items they tried to steal. Mostly the shoplifters concentrated on small expensive items. Although nobody knew exactly how much food was stolen from supermarkets annually, reporter Bill Fay estimated the amount conservatively at one-fifth of one percent of total sales, making the total $22 million. Supermarkets had a reported profit margin of one percent. "Most foodlifters start out modestly by stealing something small — usually a quarter pound of butter," said the detective. He made all his arrests outside the store because "legally, she wasn't guilty of larceny until she left the store." In this chain the detectives worked in pairs so a suspect could be kept under constant surveillance until she left the store. Even if they lost sight of a suspect for a few seconds in an aisle they might pass up an apprehension due to worry about a false arrest charge, if the suspect got suspicious and ditched the goods. Of those he apprehended he commented: "Strangely enough, their stories are always the same. It's always the first time they stole anything, and they'll never, never do it again. Maybe I'm cynical, but I don't think I've ever caught a first-time foodlifter."[3]

When apprehended, if the total of stolen items was small, say one or two items worth less than $1, this Chicago chain let the shoplifter go with a stern warning, after the person signed a statement acknowledging the theft. Signed statements went into the company's permanent files. If the person was caught again the retailer took her to court and pressed charges. About 90 percent of those apprehended were women. "We operate on the theory that one good scare should reform relatively inexperienced one-or-two-item foodlifters. However, there is no percentage in trying to frighten a foodlifter once she had graduated to the four-or-five-item class. Only one threat — the fear of going to jail — impresses hardened foodlifters." Usually a first charge brought a suspended sentence but it was not uncommon for a second charge to bring a sentence of six months. Five o'clock was a popular time for foodlifters for two reasons. For one thing the cashiers were really busy; for another the manager was usually in his office looking at the daily receipts.[4]

Just a few months later the New York *Journal of Commerce* estimated that pilferers walked out with a daily haul of $200,000 from United States supermarkets. Based on a six-day week that would be over $60 million annually. A detective with a large supermarket chain in Ontario, Canada, related what he looked for in the way of suspicious behavior. For him one dodge was when a shopper opened her handbag, took out her change purse and put it in her pocket, then pulled out her change purse instead of opening her handbag at the checkstand. This type of behavior was considered a giveaway to store detectives since it led them to believe the woman was stashing items in her handbag. Also, shoplifters were invariably furtive, casting darting glances at the manager and other store employees. This Canadian chain also followed the practice of taking those apprehended into the office and scaring them. Some Canadian supermarkets relied on that method alone, refusing to prosecute. In court first offenders usually got off with a fine of $10 or $25. For repeated offenses the sentence was 30 days in jail. None of the stores liked sending shoplifters to jail, observed the detective, "because they feel it adds up to bad public relations."[5]

When *Business Week* assessed the situation in 1952, it said that some stores were claiming that shoplifting had increased 25 to 50 percent in the previous year. Admitting no one knew how much was taken, it decided the rate of shoplifting went from a low of one-quarter of one percent up to a high of one or 1.5 percent of total sales. Food retailers put it at the low end of the range while department and drug stores placed it at around one percent. A Boston supermarket executive noted that "we'd be out of business if we lost as much as 1%." Offenders were mostly females and amateurs with estimates that 70 percent of those apprehended were first-time offenders. Kleptomaniacs were less than one percent. A Houston protective agency declared that 95 percent of apprehended shoplifters could afford to pay for the items they tried to steal. Although it then said that a "fair number" of those apprehended were low-income people.[6]

While no evidence was cited to support the idea there had been a large increase in shoplifting in the past year, *Business Week* went on nevertheless to try and explain it. Retailers were said to put the blame for the increase on three factors: the growth of self-service selling, the rising cost of living, and "the peculiar psychological temper of our times." Some were shoplifting not just because prices were high but because they were mad at the high prices, and because they were keeping up with the Joneses. "Some observers feel the reason is a general breakdown in morale after the war. Life has suddenly turned humdrum, the pilfering breaks the monotony. Women culprits complain they have marital troubles, need distraction." A Richmond, Virginia, retailer gave it all an inscrutable political cast when he declared, "Those scandals in Washington have a lot to do with it." From Cleveland, Ohio, a merchant stated that "Everyone has come to expect something for nothing." Another cause mentioned was inefficient personnel. A lot of stores were checking with mirrors. Regarding apprehensions, one retailer said he'd rather lose the merchandise than lose good customers. Retailers continued to worry about false arrest problems and in general were loath to create an "intimidating atmosphere." A San Francisco department store reported that it let 80 percent of its offenders go free.[7]

Store detective Amelia de Santis claimed in 1955 that $250 million was stolen annually from American department, drug, and food stores—a significant advance over previous numbers. According to this account, professionals were responsible for just 17 percent of the loss. She said that, of the amateur shoplifters, "only a small number are apprehended with retailers considering prevention and protection to be more important than apprehension." New York's SMPA still remained active in the battle. De Santis argued that the "quiet" apprehension of shoplifters had been developed because stores demanded it. A "scene" could drive customers away from the store, never to come back. Moreover, a fight raised the chance of costly litigation, and the ever-present nightmare of false arrest action. For de Santis, shoplifters came from all groups, regardless of class, age, or race. She made no mention at all of gender.[8]

Around the same time, a Canadian source put that country's shoplifting loss at $50 million a year. The general average was about 0.5 percent of gross sales, with losses for big food stores believed to range from 0.5 to 1.5 percent. While the account claimed there was no average shoplifter, it quoted a private protective agency as saying that "the highest incidence of shoplifting occurs in the more depressed areas where there are a lot of rooming houses, small hotels, etc." It was one of the few comments to specifically single out the lower classes as major shoplifters.[9]

It was only in the 1950s that children were first mentioned as a problem for retailers. Late in 1951, the public schools in Tacoma, Washington, sent a letter to the parents of all junior and senior high school pupils requesting their help in stemming the tide of shoplifting. Reportedly, children in the 7 to 12 age group were common offenders. As to their motivation, said Dr. Paul Kaufman, lecturer in psychology at Tacoma General Hospital's School of Nursing, "they want to gain something desirable to make up for deprivations or attain some possession that will give them increased stature in the eyes of the community." There was the desire to keep up with the juvenile Joneses, an attempt to ease anxiety or tension caused by an unhappy home situation. And "an urge to get even with someone toward whom he feels resentful.... But he hesitates to strike back at the adults who have aroused his resentment for he is dependent on them for love and approval."[10]

A 1952 account said the big new problem was juvenile shoplifters, 11 to 17 years old, with a lot of it seeming to be a matter of shoplifting for shoplifting's sake —"It's smart, and it's fun, they seem to feel." Amelia de Santis mentioned, in 1955, that there were more teenage shoplifters in the game than ever before.[11]

Retailers continued to fight back; however, they were always ambivalent about releasing many, at their discretion, or prosecuting all. When Merle Goddard took over as secretary-manager of the East Bay Grocers Association in California in 1953, he found shoplifting to be a major headache, with losses from the activity estimated at one percent of sales. For several months he and the owners of nine stores plotted action. Previously those stores had downplayed the offence. Many had been burned by adverse publicity. Their campaign against shoplifting stressed four points: to make customers realize that it was their money being stolen; that shoplifting boosted costs that had to be borne by the honest shopper; that they would drop their old scold-them-release-them policy, with grocers urged to post signs reading: "Shoplifting is a crime punishable by law." Fourthly store employees were urged to speak to each entering customer because "the shoplifter hates to be noticed." The association also urged its members to increase surveillance. And they did all over the country as technology tried to keep pace.[12]

The practice of checking bags at a retailer's door drew an angry letter to the editor in 1955 from N. Hobbes, who complained of the practice whereby stores required customers to deposit bags brought in from outside at a checking place before entering the shopping area. Specifically, he complained about the lack of actual numbered checks and the dirt that got on his bag. "I still cannot think that in a free country it is legal to take personal property into custody in such a graceless manner, nor can I see why I should trust the integrity of those who operate the store, since they obviously don't trust mine."[13]

Bamberger and Company, based in Newark, New Jersey, took delivery in May 1956 of the first of four closed-circuit television cameras that would be spotted throughout the store. In a trial store officials found that a single camera could cover almost every part of the street floor.[14]

After 13 weeks Bamberger was said to be happy, with apprehensions up 20 percent. Alexander's of New York had just installed cameras of its own while a Philadelphia department store had them on order. Estimates then were that shoplifters made off with some $100 million annually. Bamberger also expected quicker apprehensions when all 17 of its store detectives were wired for sound. Each detective would carry a one-way radio connected with a central switchboard located next to the television monitor.[15]

By 1957, engineers had invented what they called a "deflector-reflector," an adaptation of the ordinary mirror, to detect shoplifters in retail stores. Large and convex those mirrors were 26 inches in diameter.[16]

Shoplifting convictions had doubled in 20 years, reaching about 20,000 a year in 1959. That year some retailers in London, England, hired store detectives from private agencies and dressed them as Santa Clauses to patrol their stores.[17]

Life also got a little easier for retailers thanks to state lawmakers. Florida put a tough new law into effect July 1, 1954. It was a measure designed to help merchants overcome one of the most formidable obstacles in trying to protect themselves from liability for false arrest or false imprisonment. Rather than risk a suit for false arrest many shop owners reportedly often permitted shoplifters to carry off merchandise. But the new law allowed a merchant or his employee to take a suspect into custody for a "reasonable length of time" in an attempt to recover the goods. Even though the merchant made a mistake, he could not be sued successfully if he could satisfy a court that he had a "probable cause" for acting as he did. Lobbying successfully for the law was the state Chamber of Commerce's Retail Merchants Division. Lawyers for retailers held that the probable cause test eliminated the danger of arbitrary action by the stores and protected the shopper from unreasonable detention or arrest. The Florida State Retail Association told its members, "we must avoid irrational procedures that would ruffle customer dignity, injure customer goodwill, and even incite a legal attack on the new law."[18]

Less than four years later six other states — Arizona, Pennsylvania, West Virginia, Ohio, Illinois, and Kentucky — had also passed laws, said *Time* magazine, "to make arrests of suspected shoplifters easier." Of course, those laws did not make arrests easier or harder. What they did was to make it easier for retailers to avoid liability for any wrongful actions. At this time it was reported that shoplifting removed at least $250 million worth of goods from United States supermarkets each year.[19]

One of the few voices raised to point out that all stock shrinkage wasn't due to shoplifting was that of business writer E. B. Weiss. He noted in 1958 that he had been pointing out for years that the retailer tended to blame total stock shortage on the shopper. And he had been explaining for the same long period of time that, actually, the shopper was the smallest culprit in the shrinkage situation. For him there were two real factors. One was the retail merchant himself, through poor management practices, poor supervision, poor personnel practices, and so forth. And, "store employees of all ranks out-steal the shopper to such a degree as to put the shopper out of the running completely as a factor in stock shortages." According to a company that specialized in auditing stock shortages, "malpractice by other than rank-and-file employees in retailing may be responsible for more pilferage than the huge pilferage rate of the rank-and-filers." Weiss added that the shortage rate in branches of some department stores was quite staggering but the shopper's contribution to that severe loss was minor. He called for a detailed study of shoplifting to determine what part each factor played. "If shopper pilferage were totally eliminated it would hardly make a dent in the total shortage factor!.... Store employees of all ranks out-steal the shopper," he concluded.[20]

A few months later, Weiss made the same points again in another article. This time he declared that for every $1 pilfered by the shopper, stores were losing $15 through other causes of stock shortages. That discovery was made, he said, because in recent years special auditing firms had developed and delivered to retailers newly discovered techniques for uncovering causes of stock shortages. However, he gave no details as to how an audit distinguished between a shoplifted item and one stolen by a clerk.[21]

At a 1959 bookstore owners' convention there was a panel discussion about shrinkage at college bookstores, many of which were moving more and more to the self-service style. One panelist was William Alexander, a security consultant for industry and retail stores. Alexander said shortages amounted to $300 million a year in department and specialty shops. He estimated that 50 percent of all shrinkage in a store came from honest causes; for example, a book retailing for $6 was accidentally marked by the receiving department at $5, an unpriced item was brought to a cashier who guessed at the price, wrongly, and so on. Another 25 percent of shrinkage came from employee stealing while Alexander estimated shoplifters were responsible for only 25 percent of total shrinkage. Three-quarters of customer thefts were made by "the American housewife." He believed that professionals took about 25 percent of the shoplifting take.[22]

This period was marked by estimates of shoplifting totals that were all over the place. Shoplifters were sometimes described as coming from all groups of people but the female still was characterized as dominating the practice. For the first time, children (under 18), were mentioned as problem offenders. Retailers turned more and more to technological advances in an attempt to control the problem. Their lobbying efforts were successful in several states in establishing laws on the books which were designed to make it more difficult for customers to take successful legal action in the face of retailer wrongdoing. As well, retailers began to turn to outside agencies for store security. Disappearing was the retailer whose protective personnel were its own employees. Outside agencies hired to reduce shoplifting had, of course, a vested interest in finding it, and in overstating its prevalence. The notion that shrinkage was due solely to shoplifting continued to be challenged only infrequently.

Chapter 4

LATEST TEENAGE FAD: SHOPLIFTING, 1960–1969

"Pregnant women occasionally develop the mania."—*Journal of Retailing*, 1961

"The under-21 group is on the greatest shoplifting spree in our history."—*Reader's Digest*, 1967

A nationwide survey of 308 food store operators in 1961 with 2,918 outlets determined that shoplifting cost the country's food retailers 0.5 percent of gross sales, at least $260 million, "but less than many alarmists would believe." The most frequent offenders were women shopping alone, with the average theft nationwide worth $1.11, and $1.45 per theft in larger volume stores. Favorite items to lift were small packages with relatively high prices such as meats, health and beauty aids, and cigarettes. For the trade journal *Progressive Grocer* the problem "is a growing one everywhere…. Tightened laws and law enforcement are urgently needed." This survey claimed to have captured a full profile of the average shoplifter: she was in her thirties, was a lone shopper, had secreted her $1.11 worth of pilfered merchandise in her handbag or clothing, preferred to steal on Saturdays, did not need to steal, "will not be prosecuted, if caught, is increasing in numbers, represents a $260,000,000 'silent tax' on the food business."

Fully 85 percent of the surveyed stores reported a customer pilferage rate of one percent or under; 81.5 percent of those retailers said they employed no personnel specifically to deter customer pilferage. With regard to females as the most frequent culprits one operator did note that it was that way "if only because she is the most frequent shopper." The most prolific stealing groups were, in order starting with the worst: women alone, children alone, men alone, mother and children, man and wife, entire family, father and children. Of the retailers surveyed 62.3 percent cited women alone as shoplifters, 45.8 percent listed children alone, only 3.2 percent mentioned father and children.[1]

Based on the data supplied by the Kroger company's 65 supermarkets, the favorite days to shoplift were, in order: Saturday, Friday, Tuesday and Thursday (a tie), Wednesday, Monday. From Kroger data the most frequently apprehended age groups were, in order: 30 to 39 years, 11 to 20 years, 21 to 29 years, 40 to 49 years, and 50 to 59 years. Journalist Robert O'Neill wrote, "It might be said that the age group with the most representation among your shoppers will be the age group that steals most often." From the larger group of stores surveyed, 18.8 percent had checking facilities for packages brought into the store; 28 percent said they examined customers' parcels at the checkout. Of the 72 percent of retailers who did not use that technique, most felt it was effective but avoided it because it was too "controversial" a technique. One retailer commented: "We have signs up, 'We reserve the right to examine all shopping bags,' but we do it only rarely, when we're pretty sure of someone stealing." O'Neill added that "many operators consider it too drastic as a regular practice." Two-thirds of those surveyed felt shoplifting was increasing. However, some voiced the opinion that it was a reasonable cost since the customer did all the work of collecting her own groceries. That was a reference to the fact that the advent of self-service made things much cheaper and quicker for the customer, compared to prior times when a clerk had to gather all of the items. A full 75 percent of those 308 retailers reported they took no legal action against suspects. Only two percent of them, six companies, reported that they had been successfully sued for false arrest in the previous five years. The damage amounts awarded varied from $500 to $2,500. A further 12 companies volunteered the information that they had been unsuccessfully sued by shoplifters.[2]

Britain's Institute for the Study and Treatment of Delinquency released a report in 1962 in which it said the average British shoplifter was a female between the ages of 51 and 60 who had enough money to pay for the goods and who had not been in trouble before. Lately she had been a foreign-born woman. Men pilfered half as often as women and half the men were arrested for book stealing, which was almost unknown among women. As for motivation the report said more women were driven to shoplifting through depression than from kleptomania. For these perpetrators the offense was often considered to be "a miniature suicidal attempt."[3]

Kleptomania made a brief return in 1961 when a trade journal commented that it was true that a good part of shoplifting was done by juveniles and kleptomaniacs. The kleptomaniac was hard to identify on sight "as she, for they are almost always middle-aged married women, appears to be a respectable shopper."[4]

Writing that same year in the more scholarly *Journal of Retailing* were ex-policeman Thomas Fitzmaurice and retail analyst Herman Radolf who observed that kleptomania also figured in the shoplifting problem and that the compulsion to steal occurred in the most unsuspected individuals. "Pregnant women occasionally develop the mania. In some cases the kleptomaniac may be a mature woman with grown children and a background of complete respectability in both her family and community life," they wrote. In conclusion the pair said that "normally honest housewives who feel temporarily frustrated in career ambitions, or women who feel deprived at the menopause because of not having children, may suddenly yield to the compulsion that drives the kleptomaniac." After that little flurry the concept vanished again.[5]

A 1963 estimate declared that in supermarkets, one out of every 52 emerging customers had shoplifted something. It was stated to be even more prevalent than that in variety stores. Total take from supermarkets was then said to total about $280 million per year, with another sum equal to that amount being shoplifted from all other retail outlets combined — department stores, drug stores, apparel shops, and so on. While reporter Don Wharton admitted that no one knew the exact cost of pilfering he felt comfortable in estimating over half a billion dollars annually, plus another huge expense for store protection, guards, lawyers, special packaging, and technical equipment. The same shoplifting pattern was said to exist in other nations such as Britain, Canada, France, Germany, Italy, and Scandinavia. In all those places, and America, shoplifting was undergoing an upsurge. Wharton attributed this to the advent and expansion of self-service stores and the problems associated with improved display techniques which were psychologically designed to increase impulse buying. Said one manager, "We try to tempt people into buying and we tempt them into stealing." All too often the standard assumption was that all could be set right by paying for the stolen goods. Out of 6,500 people who confessed to shoplifting in 1962 in Alexander's New York stores, 3,500 were teenagers, most of them girls. Shillito's department store in Cincinnati determined that 78 out of every 100 of its shoplifters were under 18, 45 girls and 33 boys. Wharton went on to estimate that between 15 and 20 percent of shoplifters were professionals. The 75 to 80 percent who were amateurs — two-thirds of which were females — were said to come from all economic classes.[6]

Estimates skyrocketed again when *Progressive Grocer* said that in 1965, shoplifting would cost American merchants more than $2 billion. Ten percent of the pilferers were said to be professionals. Describing the main perpetrator, the trade journal declared, "The fastest and boldest hands in the nation are the same hands that rock the cradle, do the laundry, cook the family meals, and wield the gavel at the PTA meeting. They belong to the average American housewife who this year will steal more than all the nation's burglars and hold-up men. She does about 90 percent of the nation's shopping and about 85 percent of the nation's shoplifting." Of course, if that were true it would make females underrepresented among shoplifters. However, by that time women no longer did that high a proportion of the shopping.[7]

Adding to the idea of a drastic increase in shoplifting was a 1965 report from the FBI stating that shoplifting was the nation's fastest growing form of larceny, having increased 93 percent in the previous five years. During 1964 police in America recorded 184,473 shoplifting cases, involving goods worth almost $5 million. Most shoplifters were women, said the FBI, probably "because of the ease with which the female shoplifter can conceal stolen articles on and around her person."[8]

Such reports added fuel to the fire and caused some accounts to adopt an almost hysterical tone. Late in 1966 *U.S. News & World Report* stated that many merchants called it the worst year they could remember for shoplifting. The estimate given for 1966 was the $2 billion figure. Seeking to explain the reasons for the increase the article cited the usual reasons such as the spread of self-service and flashy displays. However, it added, "But the overriding reason for the rise in thievery was described in a typical comment by a security officer of a Houston store, as 'a gradual moral breakdown and lack of respect for others.'"[9]

Writing in *Good Housekeeping* a year later, Fredelle Maynard cited one security expert as claiming that shoplifting had become "a way of life on the American scene." About every 30 seconds over the previous year somebody was said to have been arrested for stealing, usually in a retail store. And nobody knew how many got away with their loot, "from 5 to 200 times as many as are caught." Shoplifting was practiced by "respectable" people — it was not seen as a real crime, but in a gray area. Looking for the reasons behind this rise in "small-scale dishonesty," Maynard also cited the usual causes, such as spread of self-service, although she claimed there was essentially no self-service at all as recently as 1937. However, Maynard declared, "More important than these physical inducements to shoplifting is a kind of moral air pollution that beclouds like smog the American conscience." This may have been the first article to tag the practice with one of its more catchy nicknames—"the five-finger discount." In Maynard's view shoplifters were made up of one percent kleptomaniacs, nine percent professionals, with the remaining 90 percent falling into two groups, amateurs and juveniles. Agreeing that the typical amateur was a woman, this reporter was quick to add that "this doesn't mean that women are more larcenous than men, but only that they do more of the shopping." For her the most striking secret development on the shoplifting scene was "the alarming increase in the number of teenage thieves."[10]

If the reasons for shoplifting were in dispute, Maynard declared that "there's agreement that it's on the increase." She helped that along by citing that estimated yearly losses from shoplifting cost retailers $2 to $3 billion, a significant increase over $2 billion, but she did not cite supporting data. All this was going on despite the rash of security measures instituted over the previous 10 or so years. Measures such as stores built with no, or less, blind spots; small items stapled to large cards or encased in plastic bubbles; rest rooms, phone booths and locker areas unobtrusively policed by wide-angle mirrors and hidden peepholes; one-way vision mirrors in dressing rooms; plainclothes store detectives; uniformed security; closed-circuit television. As well, there was an increased use by retailers of outside security firms, all of whom had a vested interest in finding more and more shoplifting. Merchants were said to then be more into prosecution of offenders rather than just letting them go with a warning. Noted also was the fact that many states had enacted laws which made the willful concealment of merchandise a crime, even if the customer had not left the store with the concealed goods. By this time a United States Supreme Court decision had upheld the storekeeper's right to reasonable detention and questioning of any suspect.

Exactly how much shoplifting (and protection to combat it) cost the consumer was impossible to estimate. Still, security industry expert John Lynch told a convention that product prices could be reduced by 10 percent if proper security safeguards were maintained. Maynard expressed more concern over the cost of shoplifting in human terms. She, and others, often pointed out that the shoplifter who stole a 98 cent lipstick would not dream of stealing 98 cents from an open, unwatched cash register. Maynard spoke of the cost in terms of "the erosion of values and standards, the spread of moral disease." One store manager spoke for all concerned Americans, she thought, when he remarked that "the tragedy of the current shoplifting problem in this country is not so much what happens to the victims. It is what happens to the thieves."[11]

Life magazine reported in 1967 that the shoplifting total was $2 billion annually, double the amount of seven years earlier. Only five percent of the lifters were professionals. "Most, in fact, are housewives." For them shoplifting was explained as a way of picking up little luxuries which could not be rationalized in their budgets. Other factors were the desire for the thrill of getting something for nothing or taking revenge on a hostile, impersonal world. A store manager estimated that for every shoplifter who was apprehended, 59 escaped. According to this account, about half of all shoplifting was done by teenagers, "many of whom picked up techniques from their mothers." Kansas State University criminology professor Joseph Rogers explained that normal law-abiding people turned into shoplifters through an elaborate rationalization process that allowed them to neutralize their guilt feelings. For example, they thought to themselves, "How could this big store be hurt by the loss of a $5 pair of earrings?"; "A lot of other people are doing it, why not me?" They blamed the store for high prices or for slow or discourteous service, and stealing became justified retaliation.[12]

Between Thanksgiving and Christmas 1967, there were four million cases of shoplifting, said Saul Astor, president of Management Safeguards Inc. That had an associated cost of $500 million, with the yearly total still listed as $2 billion. A major department store with sales of $800 million annually spent an estimated $3 million on security; a discount chain grossing $300 million spent $1.5 million. In this account, reasons for the increase in shoplifting included moral decay, more drug addicts, and — the most important reason of all — the rising popularity of discount stores, which were even more short-staffed than the traditional department stores. Prosecution of offenders remained a costly and time-consuming affair, as well as containing the potential to generate bad publicity. "Thus while most stores threaten prosecution, more often than not they send shoplifters away with only a tongue lashing," observed *Business Week*. It meant that managers often regarded their sales staff as the first line of defense. However, said one security consultant, "an alert, knowledgeable sales staff is something you can't get any more." Some security managers regarded the sales staff itself as a prime source of trouble, especially during the busy holiday season. One expert was quoted as saying, "Part-time people don't have much of a stake in permanent store work, no loyalty to the company, so they just lift the stuff." If store employees were indeed less attentive and vigilant than in the past it may have had something to do with the then ongoing changes to the position of retail clerk. Where once it had been a career possibility, with benefits, steady wages, and so forth, more and more the positions were temporary, part-time, and having no benefits and a declining relative wage.[13]

A trade journal, *Modern Packaging*, reported in 1968 that a yearly loss to shoplifting of $2 to $3 billion was probably a realistic estimate, with guesses varying from $1 to $3 billion, with a few as high as $7 billion. They also used the contemporary standard figure that shoplifting had doubled since 1960. The practice added about one to five percent to the price of retail merchandise, although it noted that employee theft added another 10 percent to prices. The latter cost more because the average employee theft was $125, compared to $3 to $5 for amateur shoplifters and $27 for professionals. A survey of 100 discount stores determined that retailers spent an average of $485 monthly on guards, who arrested only 11 shoplifters and recovered $57 in merchandise per month. In light of those findings, *Modern Packaging* concluded, not surprisingly, that "the deterrent value of more-secure packaging deserves attention."[14]

Time investigated the reasons behind the rise in shoplifting in 1968, although it did not bother to document any such rise. It did no good to ask the culprit, thought the news magazine, because one standard reply was that the person was working on an article about shoplifting and wanted to pull only one job in order to write with authority. In years past, people apprehended in stores for shoplifting often broke into tears and begged for leniency, but not today, asserted the article. According to the security manager of a State Street store in Chicago, "Their attitude now is one of hostility and belligerence."[15]

During the space of less than three weeks in December 1969, three widely read news magazines published wildly different estimates of the offence. *Life* said retailers would have a shrinkage loss that year of $500 million. This was a huge drop from other, recent estimates. *U.S. News & World Report* declared the total would be $2.5 billion with $600 million of that taken at the Christmas season. Shoplifters were said to be stealing more goods from stores than ever before.[16]

Finally, *Newsweek* stated the haul would be $3 billion. They also stated that one percent of the United States population were shoplifters, a staggering two million people. They insisted that where stores once maintained a policy of letting most shoplifters go after a tongue-lashing, they were now much more inclined to prosecute. Yet in the same paragraph it went on to say that only 10 percent of those caught were tried. Summing up the article was a San Francisco retailer who commented, "To most people, shoplifting just isn't a crime."[17]

If there were huge inconsistencies in trying to put a number on shoplifting losses, there was a consistency in the 1960s in the perception of the involvement of young people in the offence; they were engaged in shoplifting in large numbers, numbers that were rapidly escalating, and it all signaled some sort of moral decline. Toronto, Ontario, reported in 1961 that the latest teen fad was shoplifting. Kids had to steal an item, usually from a department store, as an initiation rite to join a gang. One department store, Honest Ed's, said it lost $50,000 worth of merchandise a year to shoplifters, two-thirds of whom were juveniles. There was said to be general agreement that the main cause was parents who did not take enough interest in their children.[18]

Reporter Earl Selby called youthful shoplifting a "national epidemic" in a 1967 *Reader's Digest* piece. Noting that in 1965 nearly 200,000 people were formally arrested for store pilferage and as many as 800,000 (even millions) more may have been apprehended but not arrested, Selby went on to note that "everywhere I went the story was the same: the under-21 group is on the greatest shoplifting spree in our history." According to security consultant S. J. Curts there were more than 150,000 shopliftings a week with the loss estimated at $1 to $3 billion yearly. Curts believed juveniles made up at least 50 percent of the pilferers. Arguing that youngsters rarely stole out of economic need he gave the usual reasons that they were motivated by kicks, impulse, keeping up with the crowd, and so forth. Another explanation offered was that many kids had never been taught to think of the practice as a crime — or of themselves as criminals when they stole in stores. To them it was more like a sport. If in the past, store personnel apprehending youths were met with a shower of tears, in the 60s it was more likely to be a legal pronouncement — "I want a lawyer. I'm a juvenile, you can't touch me." Selby declared that while department stores expected an annual shrinkage rate of about two percent, a shoplifting epidemic could increase those losses to five or six percent. To bring home the impact of the practice, Selby argued that if a supermarket operated on a one percent profit margin it needed $500 in extra sales to make up the loss on a $5 shoplift.[19]

That same year Fredelle Maynard remarked on the alarming increase in teenage shoplifters, saying that, for the most part, such theft was "arrogantly, self-consciously anti-adult, a thumbing of the nose at all those values that so many children associate with their parents — property, respectability, the middle-class virtues of honesty and thrift." William Phipps, of the Boston Retail Trade Board, added, "you have a society which is far more permissive than the one in which today's parents grew up."[20]

A year later, in *Saturday Evening Post* Bill Davidson wrote that there were about 100,000 teenage shopliftings a week, compared with only a few thousand a decade earlier. That worked out to 15,000 a day. Of shoplifters in total, Davidson said that most experts would tell you that over half of those perpetrators were teens, "the great majority of them white, and from middle-class suburban families." Beverly Hills, California, Municipal Court Judge Leonard Wolf described it as "the phenomenon of the teenage thrill thief. Most of these kids have plenty of money. They steal just for the hell of it — the way they smoke pot. But to me it's more serious than pot, because it's an indication of how their moral values have decayed." The gender gap remained alive since the typical teen shoplifter in America was a girl. In fact, girls outnumbered boys by about 20 to one "presumably because the young female devotes considerably more time to legal shopping too." As in other articles, this one also referred to a "current epidemic" of teen shoplifting. With regard to motivation, Dr. Chaytor Mason, a Los Angeles clinical psychologist advanced a theory: "It's part of today's widespread rebellion by our youth. Some kids express their dissatisfaction with adult society by taking drugs or becoming hippies. But many turn to shoplifting, which they think is safer and less radical."[21]

In order to combat what it saw as an alarming trend in the rise in teen pilfering, the New York–based National Retail Merchants Association was distributing in 1968 millions of copies of its seven-page pamphlet directed at teenagers and titled: "Teen-agers Beware! Shoplifting is Stealing." As well, this group had also produced a 25-minute 16mm sound film on the causes and prevention of retail inventory shrinkage. It was sold to retailers to show to their staffs. According to this organization the 1967 figure for inventory shrinkage was 1.5 percent, with department stores at 1.63 percent, and specialty retailers at 1.48 percent.[22]

Dorothy Crowe was a store detective in the early 1960s and had been for years, mostly in the San Francisco area. Of the people she arrested, 83 percent were housewives or juveniles. While she had made thousands of arrests during her career, only about four percent were actually taken to court and convicted. And all of them had priors for shoplifting. Speaking of the technical devices used in the fight against the problem, such as video surveillance, mirrors, and so on, Crowe commented that "these and other scientific aids are virtually useless. It strikes me as sheer irony that a big store will catch hundreds of housewife shoplifters, get their confessions and then let them go because they are charge-account customers who always paid their bills, and who will probably continue to use their charge plates or credit cards." In her mind, a crackdown was needed.[23]

The *Journal of Retailing* argued that a suspect could be apprehended before she left the store and that someone who was seen by witnesses to drop the merchandise before leaving the store could be held for questioning. If a suspect was released and not charged, retailers were advised to have those suspects sign statements admitting to the facts of the questioning because "such action not only provides a record for future use, but protects the store against the possibility of a false arrest suit."[24]

In London, Ontario, in November 1968, the city's two provincial judges began sending all convicted shoplifters to jail. Sixteen were jailed in one week — a housewife was sent to county jail for 10 days for stealing two pairs of children's socks. Merchants applauded this get-tough approach because, for one thing, they believed fines were not a deterrent. However, the public was upset with the approach, and it generated a lot of angry calls to radio talk shows and outraged letters to the editor. A merchants' association president admitted that "merchandising methods go so far toward making the shopper feel the items on display are his for so little inconvenience that he yields easily to temptation."[25]

Laws continued to be enacted to assist retailers, but they did not seem to reduce the prevalence of the problem. Police in New York City arrested 3,177 shoplifters in 1963; in 1962 they arrested 3,061. Alexander's personnel picked up 6,200 pilferers in its two Bronx stores in 1963, against 4,900 in 1962. This gave some indication of how few suspects were actually formally arrested by the police. Reporter Emanuel Perlmutter observed in 1964 that despite the use of high-tech items, pilfering from retail outlets reached a total of $2 to $3 billion in 1963: "Although 48 states have enacted laws in the last 10 years to help merchants fight shoplifting, thefts increase every year."[26]

Thus, in less than a decade from the enactment of that first Florida statute, almost every state in the union had some type of state shoplifting law on its books. Most of those laws made it easier for stores to take into custody suspected shoplifters for a reasonable time, in a reasonable manner, if they had reasonable grounds, and so on. The key was always the concept of "reasonable." Most of those laws made it harder for someone apprehended to sue for false arrest. Thirty-three states had laws which included protection for the merchant or his employee against false arrest. Those 48 statutes varied greatly in the punishment they prescribed, ranging from a fine of $5 and/or 10 days in jail in Rhode Island for a first offense to a fine of $10,000 and/or 10 years in jail in West Virginia, depending on the amount stolen. However, most first offenders got off with no punishment, wherever they were charged.[27]

One thing that began to happen in the 1960s was the taking of in-depth surveys to analyze shoplifting and the perpetrators. Among the first of those in-depth efforts was a survey conducted in 1965 by Ralph Head & Affiliates of New York. Questionnaires were sent to the headquarters of firms that represented over 12,000 retail supermarkets in 34 states. However, the response rate to the query was not given. Analyzed by the researchers were 7,924 cases in 1963, 8,521 in 1964. It was one of the first surveys to document the disappearance of the gender gap; the gender split was even in 1963, while in 1964, 51.5 percent of suspects were male. Also documented was the relatively young age of shoplifters, with more than 60 percent of them under 40 years of age, in both years. Eighteen to 29-year-olds led the way in 1963 with 26 percent of the suspects, 24.8 percent in 1964. For 12- to 17-year-olds the respective numbers for those years were 21.2 percent and 24.8 percent; for 30- to 39-year-olds, 14.5 percent and 12.9 percent; 40- to 49-year-olds, 12.3 percent and 10.3 percent; 50- to 59-year-olds, 8.9 percent and 7.8 percent; 60 and over, 8.8 percent and 8 percent; under 12, 5.8 percent and 8 percent. Figures don't sum to 100 as age was not indicated on some cases.[28]

The average number of items per apprehension was 3.1 in 1963, 3.7 in 1964 with the average value of merchandise per apprehension being $3.06 in 1963, $3.75 the next year. The most popular time of day to shoplift was 3:00 to 6:00 P.M., by a wide margin. In 1963, 34.7 percent of the apprehensions were made then, 35 percent in 1964. Noon to 3:00 P.M. had 23 percent of the apprehensions, 20.5 percent in 1964 while 6:00 to 9:00 P.M. had 22 percent of the captures in 1963, 22.6 the next year. All other three hour periods had under 8.4 percent in each of the studied years. In terms of most popular day of the week to shoplift, in 1963 18.8 percent of apprehensions were made on Saturday, 18.4 percent on Friday, 15.2 percent Thursday, 13.3 percent on Wednesday, 12.4 percent Sunday, 12.1 percent on Tuesday, and 9.2 percent on Monday. For 1964, Friday led the way at 17.1 percent, 16.7 percent on Thursday, 14.5 percent on Wednesday, 13.2 percent on Tuesday, 11.2 percent on Saturday and Sunday, and 9.3 percent on Monday. Apprehended suspects who were actually booked in 1963 numbered 22.3 percent; the other 77.7 percent were released by the stores without being charged. A year later little had changed: 23.5 percent booked.[29]

A couple of years later another major survey of supermarkets was undertaken. This one involved over 2,000 food stores, chains, and independents, and was conducted by the trade journal *Progressive Grocer*. Average shoplifting loss was reported as 1.2 percent of sales; the average number of shoplifting cases detected in a normal week was 8.7 cases. The number (probably average) of undetected cases was said to be 171 per week, a ratio of 20 to one. According to the data, the worst offenders were, ranked in order, women, teenagers, children, men, and professionals. Average value of shoplifted merchandise per theft was $3.05. In order of importance the worst month, day and hour for shoplifting were: December — Friday — 3:00 to 6:00 P.M.; January — Saturday — 4:00 to 6:00 P.M.; November — Thursday — 5:00 to 6:00 P.M. Average monthly cost per store for anti-shoplifting devices was $190.89. Regarding prosecuting those apprehended for shoplifting, stores surveyed reported the following: always prosecuted, 27.8 percent; occasionally prosecuted, 34 percent; seldom prosecuted, 27 percent; and never prosecuted, 17.2 percent. It does not sum to 100 because a few stores ticked more than one answer.[30]

Reporting on this survey journalist Leonard Daykin observed,

"There's no doubt that super markets take a percentage figure, chalk it up to shrinkage, and bury the amount under the heading 'operating expenses.' The end result is retail prices that have a shrinkage penalty built in across the board. If this alone could offset shoplifting, it would be a practical solution to the problem." But the very interest shown by all retailers in ways of reducing and deterring pilferage was one proof to Daykin that increasing retail prices was not the sole answer. Asked to list the most frequently detected shoplifters, women were reported by 60.7 percent of the stores polled, teens by 52.1 percent, sub-teen children by 29.2 percent, men by 14.2 percent, and professionals by 6.9 percent.[31]

Throughout the 1960s retailers turned more and more to hoped-for technological solutions to the problems. As early as 1961 an article appeared touting a new device which solved the problem of whether a suspect still had the goods on him when he left the store. Retailers always worried that the suspect may have secretly replaced the item knowing he was watched, the clerk may have made a mistake, or the suspect may have only pretended to steal the item in order to set up a lawsuit for false arrest. Those problems were all solved by an electronic sensing device known as the Sentronic wand. According to the account, "Its penetrating but harmless radio-like rays can be sensed through any type of clothing, through leather handbags, plastic briefcases and any other type of container, the manufacturer says." The only requirement was that the article had previously been given a treatment with the special chemical composition — the tracer. If a person stole such a treated item and walked through an arch (much like today's), he set off an alarm. When you purchased such an item the clerk deactivated it. Invented by E. M. Trikilis of Columbus, Ohio, president of General Nucleonics, Inc., the Sentronic-Storegard system was set to be offered to North American retailers in the fall of 1961. Expected cost for the system was around $75 per unit. One unit was necessary for each check stand. Those units were rented, not sold outright. As well, there was an installation fee and also a charge for each of the tracers. Apparently, few retailers accepted the offer because the Sentronic system quickly vanished from sight.[32]

Other methods used by retailers to combat shoplifters around this time included putting small items in big outsize cardboard packages. However, pilferers twisted them off. Next, stores moved to blister packs. In Oakland, California, police had set up a central file index carrying the names of all apprehended shoplifters "whether prosecuted or not."[33]

Despite such technological devices as closed-circuit television, electronic sensors, and so on, most Canadian retailers were described in 1963 as afraid to use them, except in special circumstances, one reason being that "they hate to use anything that will offend honest customers." One store that year had installed a concealed television camera for three days in a changing room in the dress department. During that test period 50 percent of teenage girls who went into the room were shoplifters. However, no one was prosecuted because the store didn't want to publicize the fact that it had a television camera in the changing room. Meanwhile a Canadian supermarket executive remarked that the electronic gadgets were only effective when signs were posted saying they were being used; then they worked as deterrents—"but you lose customers." Some retailers were even reluctant to use mirrors because those who did use them believed they offended some customers. One investigation firm estimated shoplifting would cost Canadian retailers $30 to $40 million worth of merchandise in a year. Investigators and retailers all agreed that shoplifting was increasing. Other estimates put the figure as high as $50 million. Said a supermarket retailer, "If you don't have it close enough to steal, you won't sell it." Mentioned as frequent offenders were teenagers, but reporter Beatrice Riddell added a qualifier: "This doesn't necessarily mean kids are worse than they used to be. But there are a lot more teen-agers." Riddell also observed that shoplifters came from all walks of life with the only generalization being that "the majority of shoplifters are women — natural enough because the majority of shoppers are women."[34]

One American store had a loudspeaker that kept repeating the warning "Put It Back." Around 1967, former Akron, Ohio, refrigeration engineer Jack Welsh devised a minute transmitter, smaller than a pencil dot, to go on price tags. Unless it was deactivated at a checkout counter, it set off alarms. However, this JKR Company system was expensive. It was leased at an annual cost of $3,500 per installation, with one unit needed at each exit point. Besides the disadvantage of high cost, retailers worried that if the system were used on small, high-turnover items it would mean a longer delay at each checkstand. Also, some worried about clerks forgetting to deactivate legitimate purchases, and those ramifications.[35]

Security expert Bob Curtis argued in 1969 that the new security devices such as convex mirrors, guards, television cameras, warning signs, and so forth had not reduced shoplifting and may have increased it. For one thing the distorted view in a convex mirror made it hard to determine if a suspect put something in his pocket or just scratched himself. Some pilferers had told Curtis that they would not shoplift in a store that did not have a convex mirror — so they could see if they were being watched. In Curtis's view uniformed guards increased shoplifting losses because, for one thing, the average pilferer knew that a store using a uniformed guard did not usually have any floor detectives who posed as customers. In addition, the store personnel may have been less alert to shoplifting danger, because they had passed responsibility for control over to the guard. Curtis argued as well that the militancy of the guard tended to trigger thefts by some people who would not ordinarily steal from the store. They viewed the guard as a hostile act by management, a way of accusing them of stealing, so they answered the threat by showing they could beat the guard. Television cameras could work the same way — they could stimulate thefts by some people who saw them as a threat by management. Signs reading "WARNING: SHOPLIFTERS WILL BE PROSECUTED TO THE FULLEST EXTENT OF THE LAW" seemed like a good idea, said Curtis, but studies showed they actually could double and even triple shoplifter thefts in a store that used them. Why was that? "Simple. They get honest customers, who were not even thinking about stealing, to think about stealing. Say, they must be having a problem with shoplifting. I wonder how difficult it would be to steal from here?" Training films for employees to help them fight thefts were also said not to work. Invariably they showed shoplifting methods and, felt Curtis, "the showing of the training film intended to help fight retail crime actually does the reverse and develops new thieves."[36]

What Curtis considered the most effective deterrent to shoplifting was for a store employee to recognize the customer — to say hello, to ask if he needed help, to offer a word about the weather, or to say something like "It's good to see you again." Anything could be said as long as the customer felt that an employee had recognized her. The average "neurotic" thief would not steal, thought Curtis, in the store that day. The same fear could be used at the checkout stand — if the cashier looked the customer in the eye and said, "Is there anything else?" Also, a customer could be forced to exit past a cashier whether or not he was making a purchase. It meant that all alternative ways of exiting the store had to be blocked off, and when a checkout aisle was not in use, Curtis advised it should also be chained off. "The average shoplifter will not steal in a store where he is forced to pass the cashier.... They want no part of a theft situation where they have to walk past an employee," he explained.[37]

The idea that shrinkage happened for reasons other than shoplifting got only a few media mentions in the 1960s. Norman Jaspan, president of Investigations Inc. (a firm that had conducted investigations of retail management for years) said in 1961 that 70 percent of all inventory shortages were the result of employees' malpractice, 25 percent by honest clerical errors and the remaining five percent resulted from shoplifting. The estimate for shrinkage that year was a total of $600 million.[38]

In her Chicago-based study of the problem, Mary Owen Cameron said that in urban department stores, a two percent loss was considered a "good figure." She observed that price markdowns also figured in shrinkage, as accounting was based on dollar value, not on units. And, "Currently, store protection personnel speak of the 'generally accepted' figure of 75 per cent of all theft as employee theft." Cameron also observed that adolescents and Blacks were kept under close observation by store security, more than for other shoppers. That bias, she believed, was unquestionably present and was a factor of some significance in influencing the selection of persons to be arrested.[39]

When a national drugstore chain gave lie detector tests to its employees, the results indicated that 74 percent of the workers had stolen goods. That caused *U.S. News & World Report* to acknowledge that employee theft may have been rising faster than shoplifting. A major cause, according to merchants, was the effects of full employment. "You've got to expect more dishonest employees as you dig deeper into the barrel," explained one.[40]

A couple of years later, *Business Week* declared that only about 30 percent of all stock shortages were attributed to customers with the rest being divided between employee theft (40 percent) and bookkeeping error (30 percent)—"accidental and planned."[41]

Saul Astor analyzed stock shortage rates in the *Journal of Retailing* in 1964. He thought the average shrinkage rate in the discount industry was about 3.6 percent while in traditional department stores it was about 1.3 percent. Shortages as a percent of retail sales hurt discounters far more than they did high-markup retailers. A one percent shortage constituted 2.7 percent of a 37 percent gross margin in a department store, but the same percent constituted about 4.2 percent of the discounter's total gross. Astor estimated that in a store generating sales of $2.5 million, about 2,500 to 3,500 shoplifters were successful per year, resulting in shortages "of about six to seven tenths of 1 percent of sales." In discount stores, he wrote, shoplifting shortages ranged from 0.5 to 0.7 percent of sales "but they sometimes climb to an excess of one percent of sales in badly-protected stores in low-income areas." Those loss rates of 0.5 to 0.7 percent were estimated to be 30 to 50 percent higher than the shoplifting losses in traditional department stores, but shoplifting losses in discount stores could be 100 to 200 percent higher than department store losses unless those discounters constantly fought the problem. The reason for higher levels in discount outlets was, explained Astor, the self-service, low-payroll concept, which resulted in sparse floor coverage. If 0.5 to 0.7 percent was the loss due to customer shoplifting, then the remainder of the 3.6 shrinkage loss (2.9 to 3.1 percent) must have been lost to employees and other non-customer problems.[42]

More psychological/sociological research was conducted into shoplifting behavior in the late 1960s. Researchers George Won and George Yamamoto studied how class position was related to shoplifting. Specifically they made the assumption that individuals of the less privileged or lower classes were proportionately much more likely to engage in that type of behavior than individuals of more privileged or higher classes. Note that this assumption contrasted almost all anecdotal reports of the past. Won and Yamamoto looked at data from the member markets of the Honolulu Supermarket Association. All were large outlets which, in the course of one year, had apprehended 493 cases of shoplifting. Of those apprehended, males were 40.6 percent, females 59.4 percent, under 19 years of age were 32 percent (people under 19 comprised 39.7 percent of the general population), 20 to 29 years were 22.6 percent (16.3 percent), 30 to 39 years were 17.5 percent (16.8 percent), 40 to 49 years were 14.9 percent (12.6 percent), 50 to 59 years were 6.9 percent (7.6 percent), 60 years and over were 6.1 percent (7 percent). Regarding the gender split, the researchers stated, "The general belief is, though not adequately proved statistically, that more women than men shop at the supermarkets." Almost half of the total shoplifters were students and housewives.[43]

When the researchers compared the shoplifters' neighborhood median family income to that of the Honolulu general population, they found that those with household incomes under $5,000 were under-represented with about five percent representation as offenders, while their representation reached 28 percent in the larger population. Highest household income bracket was $9,000 and over, which held 17.6 percent of the shoplifters, but 34.8 percent of the Honolulu population. This meant the middle-income brackets (under $9,000 but over $5,000) contained 37.2 percent of the Honolulu population, but 77.4 percent of the shoplifters. It caused the researchers to conclude that shoplifting in supermarkets was different from that which took place in department stores. They also declared that supermarket shoplifting was numerically and proportionately more a middle-income (or lower-middle socioeconomic status) phenomenon and less a lower stratum phenomenon. Their assumption of an inverse relationship between socioeconomic stratum and the incidence of shoplifting was, they wrote, not confirmed. "The appearance of offenders from the upper portion of the strata in the community in an area mainly involving low cost items raises some questions about their motivations in this type of deviant behavior."[44]

Late in 1969, six University of California students at Davis, California, spent several days shoplifting in Davis and nearby Woodland, California, as part of a psychological experiment. Police and the retailers involved knew about the experiment and cooperated. The idea was to see what store customers would do. Said student leader David Lopez, "We found people were not very observant. You could shoplift in front of them and they didn't seem to notice, or didn't want to notice." Lopez wore a suit and tie, carried a briefcase, "and took everything I wanted without being challenged." In Woodland, just 13 percent of the witnesses reported the thefts to store management, 74 percent just looked the other way, and 13 percent denied (in later discussion) having seen a theft. Numbers were quite different in Davis, where 62 percent reported the shoplifter, 35 percent did not report the incident, and three percent claimed they saw nothing.[45]

During the 1960s more precise measures and surveys of the problem were taken than ever before, generating more specific data such as favorite days of the week, favorite times of the day to shoplift. Also during this decade the problem was often presented by the media in hysterical terms, declaring it was worse than it had ever been in the past, and was increasing. While no precise figures on retail shrinkage existed, let alone the proportion attributable to shoplifting, news reports used dramatically higher figures, moving from $500 million annually to $2 to $3 billion, with no factual basis for the numbers. Retailers availed themselves of more and more technical devices, and outside agencies, to fight the problem; tagging items with an alarm-triggering device unless deactivated was only beginning. Few mentions were made anywhere about other causes of retail stock shortages. Mostly the entire shrinkage amount was laid at the feet of shoplifters. While some reports implied that offenders could come from any walk of life or income level, conventional wisdom still held that it was an offense committed disproportionately by upper- or middle-class women. The one difference was that young people under 19 were now fully identified as a major shoplifting problem, with some claiming they were most of the problem. This was the 1960s, the era of the counter-culture, and many people took the opportunity to attack rebellious youth, or "hippies" in any way they could. Often mixed into the assault was the concept of a declining morality in youth, in a general sense. Douglas Hagler, executive director of the Stores Protective Association in Los Angeles was typical of people who put much of the blame for shoplifting on teenagers. He said in 1968, "There is a changing morality among youngsters that permits shoplifting. These kids wouldn't steal from an aunt or a friend or a one-owner store. But they don't think a sweater stolen from a big chain will hurt the chain. So they just help themselves. We were taught as children that stealing is wrong. Period."[46]

Chapter 5

SHOPLIFTING COSTS STORES $0.5 BILLION A YEAR ... OR $5 BILLION ... OR $30 BILLION, 1970–1979

"For most of these women there is a powerful unconscious sexual significance in both the act of stealing and the stolen object."— Dr. David Reuben, 1970.

"But in many cases a store will lose more than twice as much of its inventory to dishonest employees as to shoplifters."— NYPD Inspector Adam Butcher, 1973

Throughout the 1970s, the under-19 shoplifter continued to be viewed as perhaps the worst shoplifting offender. Reasons given for the wave of youthful larceny tended to be the usual ones. Teens were pilfering because they were on a search for kicks or rebellion, status-seeking, suffering from poor parental supervision, tempted by open displays, in need of money to buy drugs, and so on. Also acknowledged was that the young shoplifter was a by-product of fundamental changes in American retailing attitudes, as youths were given more money to spend and more freedom to shop alone. A generation earlier almost every parent accompanied his daughter or son to the department store; retailers were said to have eyed with suspicion any child who ventured in by himself. When *Time* magazine commissioned a study conducted by pollster Louis Harris, the results indicated that 23 percent of the nation's youth — a figure double that obtained for adults— admitted they had stolen from stores.[1]

Writing in the *New York Times* in 1970, reporter Peter Hellman declared that more teens were picked up for the offence than any other age group. Although, he did note that this fact did not necessarily mean they were the largest group among shoplifters, because "teen-agers are not yet as practiced as adults in smoothing over the outward signs of dishonesty, so they often give themselves away. Store detectives also admit that they preselect the incoming customers they will watch — and since teen-agers are conspicuous, they are most often under surveillance, while older and more respectable-looking shoplifters will get more unobserved operating time."[2]

Helping to fuel the connection that shoplifting and youth go hand-in-hand were the activists of the day. Around 1970 Jerry Rubin proclaimed that shoplifting was a legitimate act against the capitalist establishment. Similarly, a year or so later, Abbie Hoffman advocated shoplifting as a political act in his notorious and controversial publication, *Steal This Book.* For obvious reasons libraries were unable to keep copies of the book on their shelves. Reportedly, the sections of the book describing shoplifting techniques were used to train new security personnel on what they should be looking for.[3]

If youth was still tied to the practice, the kleptomaniac was nowhere to be found. Hellman observed that everybody involved in the retailing world agreed to a man that "they claim never to have seen a so-called kleptomaniac." Other than that reference there was next to no mention of the label.[4]

Not much happened in the way of legislation, but retailers did manage to score a few victories. In New York State an amendment to the State Banking Law, intensively lobbied for by groups representing retailers, made it legal for store security employees to pick up a shoplifter in the store who had been seen to conceal goods on her person — even if she had not left the premises and, in theory, still might have paid for the goods. Apprehensions made under that law generally did not bring convictions from most judges, but it did keep shoplifters who realized they had been seen from dumping their merchandise. Store detectives could even be deputized by the city of New York if they met tough police qualifications. In that case they could make a police arrest of a shoplifter just as a regular police officer would. At the start of the 1970s all of Macy's detectives were deputized, and they went through the full procedure of formally booking and fingerprinting an accused suspect. Most retailers did not use deputized personnel because they preferred to have employees on the city payroll go through the lengthy booking procedure instead of their own. So the normal store pick-up was made as a simple citizen's arrest.[5]

A strong anti-shoplifting law was passed in 1973 by the Nevada state legislature. Maximum penalty was a fine of $5,000 and 10 years in prison. The right of reasonable detention was given to retailers as well as freedom from criminal and civil liability for that detention. A retailer who placed notice of the law in the store could bring both a criminal and civil action against a shoplifter. The retailer could bring a lawsuit against an adult or against the parents of a juvenile thief. It marked the beginning of a trend whereby store owners would try and recover money from shoplifters. California had a new law in effect in 1977 which permitted merchants to detain a suspected shoplifter when they "reasonably believed" the person was trying to steal merchandise. It also provided a mandatory fine of from $50 to $1,000 for each such violation and held the parent or guardian responsible for up to $500 if a minor was involved.[6]

From time to time the law came down hard on offenders. British magistrates started to get tough with shoplifters in the summer of 1973. Over the course of two or three weeks about 20 were jailed, usually receiving 30-day sentences. Others were fined up to $1,000. At the time about 80 percent of all convicted shoplifters in Britain were foreigners. Estimates were that British shops lost more than $700 million a year in shrinkage.[7]

The range of numbers given to shoplifting losses were varied in the extreme, just in the first few months of 1970. *American Druggist* estimated the loss that year due to shoplifting would be $600 million, up from $500 million the previous year. That was a remarkably low number, given the usual guesses. This trade journal argued the average value of goods stolen was $28 per theft, multiplied by the one out of every 60 customers who stole from a store.[8]

Just six weeks later *U.S. News & World Report* announced that shoplifting in all sections of the country was going up at an alarming rate, "contributing to the rise in prices honest people pay for the goods they buy." Their yearly total was $3 billion, a familiar number from the 1960s. Also announced was that a crackdown was beginning, with more arrests and more retailers prosecuting, although admittedly, no way had been found to halt the increase in shoplifting. Ominously, it was reported that a survey of 1,000 high school students in Delaware revealed that almost 50 percent had stolen at least once.[9]

Two weeks later the *New York Times* reported shoplifting losses would be $2 billion and that, were it not for theft, retailers "could reduce prices across the board by 15 per cent."[10]

Business Week declared in the summer of 1970 that shrinkage was pushing $3 billion a year and had jumped 150 percent since 1960. Losses at some retailers were said to be as high as four to five percent of gross sales. Adding more hysteria to the article was the thought that retailers were sparing almost no effort or expense to catch a thief; that is, they were buying more technical equipment, hiring more uniformed store guards and more plainclothes store detectives. Acknowledged in this article was that employees accounted for 30 to 40 percent of inventory shortages. For some six months, Management Safeguards Inc., a New York–based security and protection company had conducted a survey. They staked out a midtown Manhattan department store, and 500 shoppers— picked at random — were followed from the moment they entered the store to the time they left. A total of 42 shoppers, one out of 12, shoplifted something. Broken down into categories it was one out of every 10.7 females, one out of every 15.6 males, one out of every 12 Caucasians, and one of every 11.6 Blacks. Taken by the 42 shoplifters was merchandise worth a total of $300, about $7.15 each. With a 1:12 ratio, the store could expect to lose 60 cents for each shopper each day. The company repeated its survey in Boston, where the ratio was 1:20; in Philadelphia, where the ratio was 1:10; and finally returned to New York City for a second test, which also yielded a 1:12 ratio.[11]

A return to the confessional morality article was also a feature of the 1970s. *Good Housekeeping* featured a piece wherein a woman happened to see her favorite teenage niece, and the youth's friend, steal a scarf from a store. Wondering whether or not she should tell the parents what she had witnessed she decided not to, after much moral anguish. Deciding on a different course of action, the aunt had a heart-to-heart talk with the niece, hoping it would do the trick. A few days later the girl told her aunt that her teenage pal from the first incident was caught shoplifting. Thus, the niece had learned her lesson and would lift no more. During their talk, the girl related that her mother wasn't paying much attention to her.[12]

One of the well-known people who addressed the problem was Dr. David Reuben, a favorite pop psychologist of the day. Writing in *McCalls*, he said that all shoplifting fell into two categories— stealing for fun and stealing for profit. In the latter group were the professionals and the drug addicts. However, it was a small group, since the overwhelming majority were amateurs who stole primarily for the fun of it. As to how pilfering could be fun Reuben replied, "For people who suffer from certain types of emotion problems, shoplifting seems to provide a unique gratification. To a normal individual, even the idea of pilfering from a store is disturbing; to many neurotics, it is fun." When he was asked how the compulsion worked the doctor observed that most amateur store thieves were married women between 35 and 55 and had serious emotional conflicts. A close examination of their lives revealed many elements in common: "unhappy marriages, obesity, depression. Their sexual relationships with their husbands range from unsatisfactory to nonexistent. In effect, their lives have been drained of all emotional satisfaction. Most of them have been devoted shoppers all their lives—an afternoon roaming through a department store is a substitute for social relationships with other human beings." That first shoplifting episode gave them an acute emotional reaction. At one time the majority of pilferers probably fit the age and gender profile Reuben outlined, but not at the time he wrote, and probably not for several decades. When he tried to explain why his shoplifters felt that way Reuben noted that the similarity to a sexual orgasm was not merely a coincidence: "For most of these women there is a powerful unconscious sexual significance in both the act of stealing and the stolen object.... These objects represent the love, emotional and explicitly physical, they are not receiving from their husbands." This was not a new idea; it first surfaced close to a century earlier, at the same time as kleptomania, although it had disappeared completely, until raised again by Reuben.[13]

According to Reuben those amateur shoplifters were consciously afraid of being caught but unconsciously many of them seemed to enjoy the dangers involved in stealing. For most of these women, sex itself was forbidden and alluring, Reuben thought, since they saw it as a situation where a woman was exploited by a man. When they used shoplifting as a sexual substitute, the experience of being trapped by a store detective, confronted with their crime, and exposed to the risk of arrest and conviction gave them "deep emotional gratification." He did acknowledge there were some male shoplifters with emotional problems but claimed they were outnumbered 20 to one by females. Those few men who stole for emotional reasons "tend to be effeminate in character and appearance." With regard to pilferers who were teenage girls, Reuben said that when they were questioned about their reasons for stealing, all of them expressed strong resentment against the Establishment. Those kids grew up with the concept that jewelry and clothing were interchangeable with love and understanding. That came about from indulgent parents. If the parents stopped that indulgence, "it doesn't take the daughter long to figure out she can supply herself with love from the glove counter or record rack." Shoplifting teenage boys were not discussed or mentioned at all, making it seem like all the supposed increase in teen stealing was by females. Reuben also felt the stores had some of the blame to bear since retailers had done everything to make the merchandise irresistible, "and some women can't resist stealing them." As to the idea of kleptomania, the psychologist thought the concept "belongs back in the grade-B movies where it originated. Shoplifting is not a disease but merely one symptom of a deep-seated emotional problem."[14]

Early in 1972 *U.S. News & World Report* announced that the shrinkage total was $3.5 billion per year, or $9 million a day. It was an estimate from the National Retail Merchants Association (NRMA). That organization also said that arrests for shoplifting were up 221 percent over the 1961 figures. Acknowledging the general confusion about retail losses, Thomas Rafferty, a vice president of the St. Louis–based May Company, said, "We really don't know what is happening in our stores. There is much conflicting information given by so-called experts. We must develop a total attack on shortages. We can't be sure just how much is caused by internal theft, shoplifting, carelessness, lack of discipline and deliberate manipulation of figures—to make the record look better."[15]

When the *New York Times* reported the $3.5 billion figure, it added that the NRMA attributed the shrinkage total to shoplifting. However, it also pointed out that the total figure excluded supermarket shrinkage. Also mentioned in the article was that Management Safeguards—the company that did the study that tried to determine pilfering base rates—declared that the total loss to shoplifters in the United States in 1971 was in the range of $60 to $100 million.[16]

Nevertheless media estimates continued to advance dramatically. In the December 1972 issue of *McCalls*, in an article about Christmas shoplifting, it was stated that retail losses reached almost $5 billion annually.[17]

Meanwhile, at the same time in Canada, yearly shrinkage was reported at $360 million, about $1 million per day, with loss ratios varying from 1 to 2 percent in a store with lots of clerks up to as much as five percent in understaffed outlets. Philip Goldman, president of Koffler Stores Ltd. (which operated the chain, Shoppers Drug Mart) declared that if all the customers and employees stopped pilfering from Canada's stores, "retail prices could drop as much as 20%." At Goldman's own Shoppers stores, the shrinkage rate was estimated by him at one percent. "Yet we'll probably make $3 million profit after taxes at the end of the year and we'll lose maybe half of that — or $1.5 million — in shrinkage," he explained. In Canadian supermarkets the average shoplifter was said to make off with $3.40 per theft, in self-service department stores the figure was $6.70, while in conventional department stores, "it's about double." According to one article, at a discount chain in that country, Miracle Mart, some 12,000 shoplifters were apprehended in 1971 but only 10 to 15 percent of them were prosecuted. This article, published in a business publication, did mention that employee theft ran about double the rate of shoplifting.[18]

Another well-known pop psychologist of the era, Dr. Joyce Brothers, offered her opinions as to why girls stole. First, though, she noted that of the few who got caught only a small number were prosecuted — usually the black and the poor. Also noted was that shoplifters from "good" homes were often protected by their families or let off the hook by stores worried about community relations. Dr. Brothers agreed that the greatest proportion of offenders were female and that most of them were young, between 13 and 19. The teenage years were a transition stage from dependence to independence when youths freed themselves from a blind acceptance of parental values. She felt that boys tended to steal cars or became involved in physically aggressive activities while girls, as a result of cultural conditioning, expressed their defiance less dramatically, many by shoplifting. For many girls, goods, in particular luxury items, were associated with love. The items most commonly taken by female shoplifters—perfume, underwear, cosmetics—argued Brothers, "have strong sexual connotations, they suggest physical or emotional gratification…. The point is the semi-sexual excitement of the act of stealing and, afterward, the thrill of having a secret bond." In the case of younger girls she thought the sexual motive took a special form; those girls were trying to steal self-confidence. She also observed that for many girls shoplifting had become a type of rite of passage and that in many communities, cutting across the income divide, shoplifting with friends was a recognized way of asserting independence from adult authority. In conclusion Brothers suggested the offence was more than a crime; it was a symptom. "It's a symptom of the struggle of young people to find a meaningful set of values to live by. It's a symptom of the extent to which material goods are used as a substitute for success and love. It's a symptom of the disaffection these young people feel for the system. Above all, it is a symptom of the feelings of insecurity and lack of relatedness so many individuals have for the present society."[19]

According to Ronald Schmidt, assistant director of investigations for Pinkerton's Inc., only 30 percent of all people would never steal under any circumstances, while 30 percent would steal under any circumstances. The remaining 40 percent would steal, given the chance.[20]

When reporter Isadore Barmash wrote a piece in 1973, he remarked that a number of merchants were stating that progress against pilfering, lasting a few years, seemed to have lost momentum and that thieves were making off with more goods—both in actual amount and as a percentage of sales—"than ever before." However, he gave no details of the supposed progress said to have taken place. Barmash then estimated shrinkage at $5 billion a year, or two percent of gross sales, and that the belief that shoplifting had increased as a result of growing drug addiction had been recently refuted by the disclosure by many retailers of rampant pilfering in suburban stores by members of moderately well-off and affluent families. Out of 1,937 alarms that went off (at Alexander's 12 department stores), 1,328 (almost 66 percent) of them did so because cashiers forgot to remove the tag.[21]

A 1973 UK report by a working party of the Home Office standing committee on crime prevention put the estimate of total losses from shoplifting and employee thefts in a range of from just under 200 million pounds Sterling to 500 million pounds Sterling. That report was scathing in its condemnation of the notion that if goods were not displayed in ways to tempt the shoplifter they would not tempt the honest customers either. As in the United States, stores did not often prosecute offenders. The report recommended that retailers should report all offenses and leave it to the police to decide whether or not to prosecute. In 1971, of the 119,281 shoplifting offenses that were known to the police, proceedings were taken in only 47,589. Still, it tended to be higher than American prosecution rates.[22]

When the Mass Retailing Institute (MRI) conducted a 1972 survey of 1,188 stores it found that 148,525 people were apprehended in those stores for shoplifting. Out of 91,000 employees, some 3,000 were arrested for inside theft. Of those customers apprehended for shoplifting, 53 percent were juveniles under 18 years of age, 47 percent were adults; 42 percent were male, 58 percent were female.[23]

When Roy McPoland penned an article for the trade journal *Stores*, he played a little loose with history when he declared that in 1949 shrinkage ran about 0.8 percent "and didn't merit the attention of management." Over the following 25 years, he argued, tolerated losses had increased 200 percent, from a traditional one percent to a "now traditional three percent, and an accompanying decrease in the percentage of net." He declared that it annoyed him as a citizen to realize that retailing, America's biggest industry, surrendered more money annually to unexplained losses than it kept in profits reapplied to the economy.[24]

Writing in the same publication in 1975, Carol Messenger said that a conservative estimate placed shoplifting losses at $5 billion annually, with an average two percent of sales volume lost to shoplifters per store. According to her, 45 percent of all such pilfering took place during the Christmas shopping season, although she provided no data to support that idea. Messenger then reported that shoplifting in Nevada had climbed to $13.2 million yearly, "making shoplifting the Number One Public Enemy within the state." Total retail sales in the state during 1973 were given as about $2.3 billion. Actually one percent of that amount worked out to $23 million, which meant that Nevada's shoplifting losses were really 0.6 percent — a considerable distance from the two percent figure Messenger had cited, and even further removed from the three percent number mentioned by McPoland. It illustrated a media tendency to throw numbers around when none existed, or to grossly exaggerate figures even when some sort of base figures were available.[25]

Another confessional/morality tale was published in the September 1976 issue of *Seventeen* magazine in the anonymous first-person account of a 19-year-old picked up for shoplifting. Titled "I'll never shoplift again," it told of the young woman being sent to the police by the retailer but given the option of taking rehabilitation courses in lieu of court, once a week for four hours, for a month. After going through the course she saw the error of her ways and reformed. As she walked past a store window full of things she wanted, she was able to declare: "I also fully realized that I had no right to them unless I could pay for them. They were a means of livelihood for other people, just as I had a means of support. Simple? Of course, and it was something I'd always known. Yet I had never really thought about it before. I knew at that moment I'd never shoplift again. Fear of being caught was bad enough, but realizing that I was stealing from other people who are just like me was even worse."[26]

A 1977 account reported on the shoplifting "epidemic" and noted that the New York stores of R. H. Macy & Co. had substantially reduced the rate of prosecution down from "100 percent," as Macy officials concluded that the policy had not worked as the deterrent it was assumed to be. They were then said to be concentrating more on prevention than apprehension. With court delays, red tape, and light sentences, Macy concluded that too many of its security personnel were tied up waiting to testify. Another retailer was prosecuting one offender in 20 — the bad ones. Still other owners claimed to be sticking to a 100 percent prosecution policy. Many stores were beefing up their security precautions by adding more devices, hiring more personnel, and expanding training programs for employees. A highly visible security presence was then considered to be a strong deterrent, "probably the best." That was a departure from the more traditional reliance on plainclothes staff. In the fiscal year ending January 31, 1977, shrinkage was said to be two percent in department stores and 2.3 percent in specialty stores— the same figures as for the previous year. Despite there being no change in the numbers, the article still spoke of an "epidemic."[27]

For Canada it was estimated that more than $330 million worth of merchandise would be shoplifted in 1977 while more than $335 million would be lost internally through employee theft, pricing error, and so on. Those figures were supplied by the Retail Council of Canada, and were said to be conservative. According to the Council's research manager, M. F. Fruitman, the belief was that shrinkage through theft was on the increase and that retailers had to do more than they had been doing to combat it. Also reported was that more than half of all the merchandise lifted (in number, as opposed to value) was stolen by teenagers, "mainly males, although retailers feel the statistics may be influenced by the comparative

ease with which teenagers are caught." To combat shoplifting it was estimated that Canadian department stores with in-house security forces
would spend that year more than $130 million on security personnel and
about $19 million more on equipment.[28]

An FBI report stated there were over 600,000 shoplifting arrests by
the police across the United States in 1976, nearly three times as many as
in 1970. At the same time the U.S. Department of Commerce estimated
merchants' losses from thefts in 1976 at some $8 billion.[29]

Perhaps the most extreme example of exaggeration, inflated numbers, and lack of supporting data or sources came in a November 1978
issue of *Nation's Business*. It reported that retail sales for 1978 could reach
an all-time high of $771.7 billion, up from the previous year's $706 billion. "The bad news is that shoplifters will siphon about four percent off
the top. Result: Retailers will incur about a $31 billion loss, and consumers
will pay higher prices." No source was cited for any of the figures. One
source in the industry put the average shrinkage rate at four percent and,
of course, not all of it was lost to shoplifters. In any event, only in the previous couple of years had the shoplifting/shrinkage totals been estimated
at as high as $5 to $8 billion annually. According to the article the reported
incidence of shoplifting rose 73 percent between 1967 and 1972, although
it didn't explain to whom that was reported. Additionally, it stated that
around four million shoplifters were apprehended each year — with the
Commerce Department listed as the source — but that only one out of
every 35 shoplifters was caught. That would bring the total number of
offenders close to half the entire population of the United States. While
this article cited the FBI statement, noted above, that the arrest rate for
shoplifting had increased threefold from 1970 to 1976, it did not mention
the actual number of 1976 arrests. For one thing, it would have called into
question its own four million figure.[30]

Late in 1979, *Business Week* reported that shoplifting drained the economy of upwards of $8 billion a year, and that this merchandise loss, cou-
pled with extra security costs, added an average of 2 to 3 percent to
retailers' costs. "In fact, shoplifting appears to be growing faster than most
segments of the economy, including the inflation rate." William E. Cobb
of the West Virginia College of Graduate Studies found that only one out
of 1,250 shoplifters ever saw the inside of a jail cell. A good part of the reason, he thought, "why the benefits are all on the side of the shoplifter is
that judges are reluctant to imprison them.... But shoplifters prey not just
on stores but on the economy as a whole."[31]

Exaggerated numbers appeared in a Canadian business periodical at
the end of 1979 when the *Financial Times of Canada* reported on the

"epidemic proportions of shoplifting in Canada" by saying it cost Canadians anywhere from $400 million to about $4 billion a year, depending on the estimates given by various "experts." From the Retail Council of Canada came an estimate of $1 million a day, while Ross Harrington, president of Loss Prevention Services, Ltd. put the number at closer to $10 million a day. Actually those numbers should be $365 million and $3.65 billion (based on a seven-day shopping week) or closer to $300 million and $3 billion (based on a six-day week, then the norm by far). Given the size differential of about 10 to one between the United States and Canada, the $4 billion translated to $40 billion in America. Annual retail sales in Canada were estimated at $77.6 billion in 1979. A first-time shoplifter in that country was usually given a suspended sentence or an absolute discharge for theft under $200.[32]

The number of shoplifting thefts known to the police in the United States were as follows, in the 1970s:

1973	349,283
1974	450,096
1975	532,656
1976	579,978
1977	607,712
1978	624,387
1979	688,494[33]

A Van Nuys, California-based company, Commercial Service Systems Inc. (CSS) conducted a 1972 survey of 632 supermarkets in Southern California. CSS collected data on 15,542 cases in which shoplifters were apprehended. Those reported cases represented an average of approximately two apprehensions per store per month. However, CSS estimated that each store in its survey was actually victimized six times a day, an estimate it called conservative. That would put the ratio at roughly one apprehension per 90 thefts. Store security people apprehended many more shoplifters than did other store employees, who had other duties. Shoplifting offenses took place on days of the week as follows: Monday, 11.9 percent of the apprehensions; Tuesday, 14.7 percent; Wednesday, 15.5 percent; Thursday, 16.3 percent; Friday, 17.2 percent; Saturday, 13.7 percent; Sunday, 10.6 percent; not indicated, 0.1 percent. Those apprehensions were made at the following time of day; before noon, 9.6 percent; noon to 3:00 P.M., 26.2 percent; 3:00 to 6:00 P.M., 37.1 percent; 6:00 to 9:00 P.M., 20.1 percent; 9:00 to midnight, 5.6 percent; after midnight, 1 percent; not indicated, 0.5 percent. As to favorite month, theft was fairly static, varying only a point or less each month from the expected value of 8.3 percent apprehended in any month.[34]

Regarding the relationship between apprehension and booking, CSS found that of the 15,542 apprehensions, 33.3 percent were booked: total males 8,509 (35.1 percent booked); total females 7,022 (31 percent); total adults 9,327 (39.4 percent); total juveniles 6,130 (23.6 percent). Of all those apprehended the survey showed 54.7 percent were male. In the adult category 50.3 percent were male, whereas among juveniles, males accounted for 61.5 percent of thefts. Age groups as a percentage of apprehensions were as follows: under 12, 9.6 percent; 12 to 17, 29.8 percent; 18 to 29, 27.1 percent; 30 to 39, 11.1 percent; 40 to 49, 7.7 percent; 50 to 59, 6.1 percent; 60 and over, 8 percent; not indicated, 0.5 percent. It meant that 66.5 percent, or two-thirds, of all shoplifting was done by people 29 and younger — at least in the type of store surveyed. The average value of recovered merchandise was $3.85 overall: $3.61 from males, $4.15 from females, $4.80 from adults, $2.36 from juveniles, $2.95 from female juveniles, and $1.99 from male juveniles.[35]

When CSS released its annual survey for 1977 it contained data from 692 supermarkets (16,255 cases), 113 drug stores (3,927 cases), and 52 discount stores (1,765 cases). They assessed professional shoplifters to be 0.6 percent of those apprehended in 1977, compared to 0.3 percent back in 1966. Juveniles (those under 18 years of age) made up 39.2 percent of the total apprehensions in 1966; they were 37.1 percent of the total in 1977. Perfect distribution by month would be 8.33 percent of the captures. It ranged from a low of 7.8 percent in December to nine percent in May. By day, perfect distribution would be 14.3 percent; it ranged from a low of 13 percent on Sunday to a high of 15 percent on both Monday and Friday. Over the 12 years the survey had been conducted, the percentage of adults prosecuted ranged from 27.6 percent in 1967 to a high of 42.6 percent in 1973; in 1977 it was 35.3 percent. Percentage of juveniles reported to the police ranged from a low of 20.4 percent in 1968 to a high of 25.8 percent in 1974; in 1977 it was 24.7 percent. While favorite month of the year and day of the week varied, but were always very close together, favorite time of the day had always been 3:00 to 6:00 P.M. It won by a large margin. The age group most often apprehended was the 12 to 17 group, every year from 1966 to 1974. From 1975 to 1977 it was the 18–29 group. Percentage of shoplifters under 30 ranged from a low of 60.8 percent in 1966 to a high of 71.6 percent in 1976; the following year it was 70.2 percent. With regard to gender the percentage of males apprehended ranged from a low of 50.3 percent in 1972 to a high of 58 percent in 1966; in 1977 it was 52.6 percent. Females were in the minority in every year of the survey. Those caught, around 80 percent in each year, concealed the stolen goods in their purse or pocket, or under their clothing. Average number of items taken per theft ranged from 3.0 to 3.2 items, over each of the surveyed years. Average value of recovered merchandise per theft moved from $3.05 in 1966 to $5.99 in 1977.[36]

CSS conducted its 16th annual shoplifting survey in 1978 when it studied data based on 17,326 cases collected from 709 supermarkets (95 percent of them in Southern California), 3,594 cases from drug stores, and 1,613 cases from discount stores. Over 70 percent of those caught were, once again, under 30. Juveniles made up 36.9 percent with children under 12 comprising 25 percent of the apprehended juveniles. Males totaled 54.9 percent, females 44.3 percent (no data for the remainder). Within the juvenile group males were 63.8 percent, females 35.6 percent. When adults were considered separately the gender split was almost equal. Prosecution of adults was 33 percent in 1978; 21.7 percent for juveniles that year. Throughout all the years of the survey, the time period 3:00 to 6:00 P.M. was the most popular with 37.5 percent of all apprehensions taking place in that period in 1978. Next most popular was the 6:00 to 9:00 P.M. period, with 24.1 percent of the captures. There was variation in the rate of prosecution/report to police by type of outlet. For the total of 17,326 supermarket cases, 29 percent of those apprehended were booked, and the other 71 percent were released with no further action. For the 3,594 drug store cases, 32.2 percent were booked; in the 1,613 discount store cases, 48.4 percent were booked. Summarizing the survey a business writer stated that, "Consequently, if time and resources require a merchant to be selective in the surveillance of potential shoplifters, his time is best spent observing the youngest customers."[37]

Battling back against shoplifting, retailers in the 1970s took a variety of steps; some were obvious, some were bizarre. As the decade began, Macy's had in its main store 48 surveillance cameras scattered around, monitored from a communications center with 12 screens in a console; their security force of detectives and guards totaled some 200 men and women.[38]

Sensormatic Electronics Corporation of Akron, Ohio, had been in business for three years, selling sensitized tag systems to be attached to goods. By mid–1970 Sensormatic had leased its system (one alarm station and 10,000 sensitized tags for $3,600 a year) to 100 merchants and manufacturers, and 40 more systems had been ordered. At the same time a rival electronic tag system, called the Knogo system, was used by about 20 retail chains. Still, this now ubiquitous technology was still very much in its infancy.[39]

Spartan Industries, Inc. was one of America's largest retailers. Among others, it operated the Korvette discount department stores. By early in

1970 it had assembled a list of about 250,000 names of confessed shoplifters and "dishonest" retail employees. It had then begun to make that list available to other retailers, as part of the services of its new loss-prevention subsidiary company. That list was said to be the only national file of its kind and the only one using computerized facilities. Names on the list were compiled from data obtained not only from department stores and discount outlets but also from supermarkets across the country. Spartan was predicting an increase in shoplifting of at least 10 percent that year. About 75 percent of the names on the list were those of shoplifters who had signed releases admitting their thefts; the rest were employees whose names were furnished by various retailing firms as having at one time admitted being responsible for a "dishonest incident."[40]

In October 1971, a joint preventive campaign was launched by the NRMA and the International Newspaper Advertising Executives— this in the wake of a report that the offense had increased 221 percent in the past decade. Because retail advertising constituted their major revenue, 700 newspapers nationwide were being asked to contribute feature articles and to run public service ads about the consequences of shoplifting. Among the points being stressed were the following: shoplifters are criminals; shoplifting not only hurts stores but "It hurts the family unit by undermining mutual trust and respect when a member is caught"; the offence not only reduces retailers' profit — it reduces the purchasing power of every customer by increasing the price of goods; shoplifting does not wreak ruin on the Establishment — "Rather it will increase surveillance, prosecution and general suspicion." An innovation in the program was said to be the program's stress on the emotional rather than the disciplinary aspects of shoplifting — the humiliation that accompanied capture. The governors of each state were made honorary chairmen in the campaign. Impetus for this approach came from the International Newspaper Advertising Executives, who introduced "community concern as the only method of decreasing the shoplifting rate."[41]

Nineteen seventy-two marked the second year for a major campaign by STEM (Shoplifters Take Everybody's Money), a broad antishoplifting drive launched the previous year by Philadelphia-area retailers. Combining public service radio, television, print, and outdoor advertising the $100,000 campaign was said to be rapidly becoming a model for merchants all over the country as retailer groups in other states were either using parts of it, or thinking of doing so. According to the account, just five years earlier retailers considered inventory shortages of one percent "disastrous," but by then the figure had jumped to two percent in Philadelphia stores. As Bernard Kant, president of Gimbel's in Philadelphia put it,

"The problem is growing and spreading like a disease." The main target of the STEM campaign was teenage offenders. In the first year, campaign television stations ran 550 free spots worth $216,000, many of them in prime evening hours; radio contributed 6,700 free spots worth $260,000. Twenty area newspapers kicked in 59,440 lines, worth about $59,570 while outdoor advertising contributed another $36,000 worth of unsold space on billboards and on posters on buses, subways, and so forth. STEM also printed up thousands of pamphlets for adults and for teens.[42]

After STEM's first year Philadelphia retailers were said to have reported decreases in stock shortages of 20 percent. Looking at that program, journalist Edward Shapson claimed it took place in an America where shoplifting cost retailers $4 billion a year, and in a Philadelphia in which shoplifting losses were estimated at $150 million yearly. Shapson felt the STEM program "confronts the prevalent anti-business feeling among many consumers, especially young people." Many of those offenders, he thought, considered "ripping off the establishment" to be an "acceptable form of social behavior." He felt the STEM approach was new as it needed "to follow strong, forceful lines, avoiding preachiness and how-to-do-it aspects of past anti-shoplifting attempts."[43]

Woodward & Lothrop, which had 13 department stores in the Washington, D.C., area, was spending about $1 million a year on security in 1972, up some 50 percent since 1969. Said Howard Haimowitz, former general manager of the National Retail Merchants Association, "Shoplifting used to be more of a taboo subject than sex or venereal disease. Many retailers denied it existed, even though it was killing them. Now they have their heads out of the sand." He felt merchants were fed up losing $10 million a day to shoplifters, and he was also certain that teenagers were the biggest culprits, accounting for over 50 percent of thefts. In downtown Cleveland, the May Company had installed 66 closed-circuit television cameras and two-way mirrors, secured merchandise under transparent plastic cubes, hired a "mod squad" of young detectives to patrol the store, and given all security personnel a 120-hour course in basic police training. Clerks were encouraged to spot shoplifters by a sliding scale of rewards, from $5 up to $1,000, depending on how much was saved in retrieved merchandise. The May Company was also testing a new kind of sensitized tag system whereby when a sale was made the clerk had to first deactivate the tag which also opened the cash drawer so the transaction could be completed. That was hoped to protect the store from false arrest suits should the clerk forget to remove or deactivate the tag, which often happened with conventional sensitized tags which were not tied to the cash drawer.[44]

Nevada kicked off a year-long antishoplifting campaign in September 1973, called "Shoplifting in Nevada is a Handful of Trouble — Don't Risk It!" Main backer of the program was the Nevada Retail Association, plus most policing agencies. Other states were said to be copying the program. After a year of the campaign Nevada merchants, responding to a statewide questionnaire, indicated by a two to one margin that their store thefts were down substantially as a result of the campaign. Around 1,400 questionnaires were mailed out; 224 were returned (16 percent). In response to a question as to whether or not actual losses were up or down from previous years, 74 merchants said down, by as much as 80 percent. The program was renewed for a second year.[45]

One novel method of prevention was supplied in 1975 by a company called Rent A Thief Canada, Ltd. For about $100 a day this company supplied an actor who tried to shoplift an item but allowed himself to be caught in the act. Security guards publicly apprehended him, yelled at him and dragged him away. It was a humiliating experience which would, it was hoped, prove to be a deterrent to all would-be thieves who caught the show. This was set against a backdrop in which it was reported that in 1974 American retailers suffered total losses of $5.8 billion resulting from crime, up from $5.2 billion in 1973, and $4.8 billion in 1971.[46]

Then there was the invention of Hal C. Becker, director of the Laboratory for Clinical and Behavioral Engineering at the Tulane University School of Engineering which used subliminal audio in an attempt to reduce shoplifting. That little black box combined music and messages in such a way that the music could be consciously heard, while the message emerged at such a low volume that it penetrated only the subconscious — or subliminal — mind. The message said, "Be honest, do not steal. I am honest. I will not steal ... if I do steal I will be caught and sent to jail." The message was on a loop and repeated itself continuously, hour after hour. Becker's "honesty reinforcement and theft deterrent system" was reported to have been at work for more than a year in at least six stores of a major chain in the New York area. According to Becker his invention cut shoplifting and employee pilferage by a dramatic 30 percent. However, since subliminal messages did not seem to work, they never became popular.[47]

Headquartered in St. Paul, Minnesota, the 3M Company introduced Tattle-Tape in 1970 to eliminate the "unauthorized borrowing" of books from libraries. It was very successful and consisted of inserting a sensitized metal strip somewhere in each book, generally out of easy sight of the reader. By the end of the 1970s the system was used by about 2,000 college, institutional, and public libraries. As well, it had also spread to bookstores. The Tattle-Tape desensitizer and sensing unit typically leased for between $1,200 and $2,400 a year, although units could be purchased out-right for $3,100 to $6,100. Tattle-Tape strips varied in price from 5 cents to 14 cents each.[48]

In September 1979, the National Coalition to Prevent Shoplifting was formed, with headquarters in Atlanta, Georgia. It was using a $245,000 federal grant to improve antishoplifting campaigns.[49]

During the 1970s a little more media attention was paid to the problem of just who was responsible for retailers' shrinkage losses. Overall, though, shoplifters still were generally given responsibility for all of it. In a 1970 account in *U.S. News & World Report* it was reported that some stores claimed that employee theft might run anywhere from five to 15 times as high as shoplifting losses. Around the same time the *New York Times* noted that shrinkage ran from 2 to 5 percent of sales, and of that total, trade estimates were that shoplifting and internal theft accounted for 60 percent with bookkeeping and human error responsible for the other 40 percent. Finally, *Stores* magazine declared that employees stole more than $2 billion a year in cash and merchandise. Later, the article cited the figure of $3 billion as the total annual shrinkage, all of it against a back-drop wherein "the always dangerous problem of shortages has risen to such unprecedented levels ... that the survival of some retailers is in doubt."[50]

While addressing an electronic engineers meeting, NYPD Deputy Inspector Adam Butcher said he was amazed at the retailers' indifference toward internal theft in contrast to their concern over shoplifting: "It's easier to blame the public than to look into your own organization. But in many cases, a store will lose more than twice as much of its inventory to dishonest employees as to shoplifters and burglars." He thought about 45 percent of shrinkage came from employees. Others thought the split was 50 percent from shoplifting, 30 percent from internal theft, and 20 percent from bookkeeping error.[51]

When the UK's Home Office did its report on crime prevention in 1973 the report noted that it considered a high proportion of losses attrib-uted by some shops to shoplifting "is really the result of thefts by their staffs and by some dirty work on deliveries." While British stores were cited for not often prosecuting shoplifters, the report complained they were even more permissive in dealing with thefts by employees, often pre-ferring to fire rather than prosecute.[52]

Back in America in 1973, both the NRMA (a trade group for depart-ment stores) and the MRI (a trade group for discount stores) reported a sharp rise in internal theft that year. Some outlets reported as high as 60 percent of their losses were due to internal sources. Shrinkage rates were said to be two percent in department stores, about 2.55 percent in discount outlets.[53]

When *Newsweek* discussed the issue in 1974, it stated retailers were then losing $4.8 billion worth of goods a year — to shoplifting and employee theft. Even when articles once in a while discussed shrinkage in a more thorough fashion, many left out the catch-all third category completely, the one containing bookkeeping error, vendor fraud, retailer malpractice, and so on. While this magazine then went on to observe that it was estimated that 75 percent of all losses were due to stealing by employees, the major focus of the article was on shoplifting. Also observed was the fact that many companies resorted to using lie-detector tests to keep their employees honest.[54]

When the *Journal of Retailing* conducted a small survey of 98 retail employees, it found exactly half of them (49) admitted to taking merchandise from their place of employment without paying for it. It caused the periodical to take the usual quote about shoplifters and shrinkage and turn it around in its opening sentence to read, "Employees steal more than 10 million dollars a day in cash and merchandise — about 3 billion dollars a year."[55]

Drug Merchandising offered an article on how to lower shoplifting in Canadian drug stores in which it said shoplifting was costing Toronto retailers an average of three percent of gross sales, and that some outlets could experience a 10 to 12 percent shoplifting loss. Although 90 percent of the article was about shoplifting, near the end it said employee theft "according to one source outshines shoplifting four to one."[56]

St. Louis–based Famous-Barr, the city's biggest retailer, had a disheartening explanation for why its losses were continually increasing. It said employees it trained to detect shoplifters "have used that knowledge to steal."[57]

According to a 1977 article in *The CPA Journal*, in a typical retail situation, in a religious articles store, shoplifting accounted for 35 percent of the inventory loss while employee theft was responsible for 55 percent. The balance of that loss (10 percent) normally resulted from a combination of order placement, order fulfillment, stock receipt, inventory record keeping errors, theft by vendor, postal service and common carrier employees, and deliberate vendor fraud.[58]

Gordon Williams of the NRMA estimated in 1977 that $500 million would be lost that year to shoplifters and $600 million more to pilfering employees. Another $400 million would be spent by merchants on loss prevention. It all cost honest customers another 2.5 percent for whatever they bought, he added.[59]

One thing that did increase dramatically in the 1970s about shoplifting was the number of studies and experiments of an academic nature conducted around the issue. One of the more intriguing research efforts was
carried out by Management Safeguard. Four large department stores in
New York, Boston, and Philadelphia were observed over the period of
August 1969 to November 1970. At random, every third person to enter a
store was followed. Of the total of 1,647 people trailed, 109 were shoplifters
(6.5 percent). Although all the stores involved had large staffs of private
detectives, only 1 of the 109 was apprehended. While the researchers kept
their random subjects under constant surveillance they did not report
shoplifters to the store personnel. With regard to characteristics of the
shoplifters, age was not a factor; of the shoppers followed who were under
21 years old, 7.1 percent stole; for those 22 to 35, seven percent pilfered;
for those over 35, six percent stole. Ages were estimated by the observers.
Race was not a significant factor; of the 1,197 whites observed, 6.3 percent
stole; of 450 Blacks, 7.3 percent shoplifted. Of the 1,075 females tailed, 7.4
percent stole; of the 572 men followed, five percent pilfered. On average
the value of items stolen per incident was $5.26. Very few people stole
more than one item while in the store. The bulk of the thefts, 94 percent,
took place on the main floor. If the researcher lost sight of a person under
observation, even for a few moments, that particular test was invalidated.[60]

A 1976 study conducted in a department store in Murfreesboro, Ten-
nessee, attempted to evaluate shoplifting preventive strategies which were
aimed at either increasing public awareness of the severity of the consequences or increasing the threat of detection. Specifically the study looked
at the effects of posting signs around an area of a department store, pointing out that shoplifting was a crime, and so forth. Results indicated that
such signs partially reduced theft rates. When merchandise that was frequently taken was identified by signs and stars, shoplifting of those items
decreased to near zero, said the researchers. In this study's background was
a claim that shoplifting had increased from $2.5 billion in 1969 to an esti-
mated $4.8 billion ($13 million per day) in 1974. Also stated was an estimate that in 1973 each American family paid $150 annually in hidden costs
due to shoplifting.[61]

Teens were the focus of a number of studies. One was a 1973 survey
done of the 930-member student body at Matawan Regional High School
in New Jersey. It was an unsigned questionnaire given to students between
the ages of 10 and 15. Fifty-three percent admitted they had shoplifted in
neighborhood stores. Of those who admitted to theft, 81 percent said they
would probably do so again. The poll indicated that, on average, the students had shoplifted at least three times; for boys the first time came at

age nine, for girls it was 10. Students said they pilfered mainly to gain items for personal use, but also for fun or "on a dare." Of the 498 boys surveyed, 61 percent said they had shoplifted; for the 432 girls the number was 45 percent. Researchers found no correlation between family income level and shoplifting; they almost always had enough money on them to pay for what they stole. If they were apprehended, the students usually told department store security personnel that they did it for kicks.[62]

When Amin El-Dirghami conducted his study in 1974, he observed that estimates of the amount of shoplifting varied from 15 to 33 percent of shrinkage, which amounted to 0.7–1.7 billion dollars per year. He attempted to measure the magnitude of shoplifting among high school and college students at a small Midwestern community to identify the characteristics of student shoplifters, and to compare the attitude of student shoplifters and nonshoplifters to shoplifting itself. From a sample of 200 college students he received 106 returned questionnaires. Of the 178 high school students in the sample 112 returned completed surveys. El-Dirghami found in the high school group 49.11 percent had never pilfered, 22.32 percent had shoplifted once, 28.57 percent had pilfered more than once. Those same figures for the college students were, respectively, 60.38 percent, 16.98 percent, and 22.64 percent. Overall, for the 218 people sampled, 54.59 percent said they had never lifted, 19.72 percent said they had done so once, 25.69 percent claimed to have shoplifted on more than one occasion. In this study no specific characteristics were identified. As well, results indicated that all groups believed that shoplifting was a form of stealing, a somewhat serious offense, and not alright for one's self or others to do.[63]

When questionnaires were administered to young adults between the ages of 14 and 28 in Honolulu, the study indicated that 28.2 percent of the respondents had shoplifted during the prior year. A total of 26.3 percent of the subjects felt retail department stores made too much money. The proportion of surveyed people who defaced property in a retail store was 28.3 percent; just over 18 percent of the respondents cheated on their income tax returns. Only 10.3 percent of those surveyed felt shoplifting increased costs to consumers. Of those who had admitted to shoplifting, 39.3 percent sold most of the stolen items; none defined themselves as narcotics users. Family members or friends knew the respondent shoplifted in 98.5 percent of the cases.[64]

Robert Kraut tried to look at the correlates of shoplifting which might influence a shopper's decision to steal, focusing on the social psychological variables suggested by deterrence. He sent out 1,500 questionnaires to a random sample of University of Pennsylvania students, receiving 606 returned surveys. From those respondents he found that 372 (61 percent) had shoplifted at least once. Of those 372 a total of 60 (16 percent) had been caught at least once. Among his shoplifters Kraut found slightly more men than women, younger students over older ones, and lower class students more than upper class ones (within the limited social class range of an ivy-league school). Religion and race were found to be unrelated to shoplifting rates. Kraut found the motivation for pilfering to be commonplace and indeed was the same as for normal shopping, "the acquisition of goods at minimum cost." He found that many people shoplifted; close to two-thirds of his sample, with one-third having done so within two years prior to data collection. One conclusion drawn was that "the consistently high correlations between a respondent's experience with shoplifting and his perception of his or her friends' approval suggest that they powerfully influence the decision to steal by providing a supportive climate." Students who shoplifted the most reported that the low risk of apprehension was an important reason for stealing and saw the least risk associated with stealing, both in terms of likelihood of apprehension and severity of formal and especially informal sanctions. Apprehension increased their estimate of formal risk.[65]

When a questionnaire was given to 106 male and 108 female high school students at a school in the northeastern U.S. in 1977, results were that 62 percent of the males and 43 percent of the females self-reported themselves as shoplifters. A significant difference.[66]

Staged shoplifting events were also a feature of 1970s studies, to assess the reactions of bystanders. Researchers at the University of Utah undertook an eight-month field study during which they staged hundreds of blatant shopliftings in two Salt Lake City drug stores to see how often the incidents were observed and reported. Follow-up interviews were conducted with witnesses outside the store. In their opening they remarked that one out of every 15 retail customers stole something, that the offense had tripled in the 1960s, and that merchants reported losing up to 50 percent of their profit — "and the consumer is expected to make up the difference." Those researchers found that the first problem in stopping shoplifting was that it was rarely noticed by other shoppers. Despite obvious actions by the fake shoplifter (who was always the same 21-year-old woman), such as reaching directly in front of the subject for items and stuffing them in her purse as the subject watched, only 28 percent of the shoppers thus exposed were judged to have noticed what she was doing. Study leaders attributed that inattention to the customers' "trance-like absorption in the task of shopping." A total of 94 subjects were exposed to the fake theft and were judged to have observed it, yet only 28 percent reported it. Thirty-eight percent of the men reported the incident, 19 percent of the women. High reporting rates were recorded for men, middle-aged people, and those with high social standing, results that tended to confirm findings by previous researchers. Further, they found that the subjects who reported the incident most frequently (67 percent of the middle-aged men with high incomes) had strong punitive feelings toward shoplifters in general. Most of those who did not report the event (57 percent of them) gave circumstantial reasons such as a clerk not being nearby, the store being too crowded, or the culprit having left too quickly. Unlike other experiments where bystanders were found to be very likely to go to the aid of a victim when no one else was around, researchers found that such good Samaritan behavior did not apply to corporate victims such as chain drug stores. Also, 41 percent of all shoppers interviewed (including those who did not observe the shoplifting) mentioned the possibility of a countersuit by the person they accused or court appearance demands as reasons they would hesitate to report a shoplifter. Concluded researchers, "the moral satisfaction gained from turning in a wrong-doer is not sufficient compensation for taking an action that may prove to be inconvenient, dangerous and time-consuming."[67]

A similar study was conducted by Darrell Steffensmeier and Robert Terry. In their staged shoplifting events they used three variables: appearance of the thief, gender of the thief, and gender of the customer. Major findings were that gender (of the thief or the customer) had little effect on reporting levels whereas the appearance of the fake shoplifter (who was rigged out either in straight, business-like attire, or in hippie garb) exerted a major independent effect on reporting levels. Assumptions made by the experimenters included the fact that research had shown that a respectable appearance served as a buffer against a deviant imputation, and that research in general indicated that women were less tolerant of deviance than were males. And traditional sex role differences, theoretically at least, had emphasized more support of stability and the ongoing system among females than among males. Thus females should be less accepting of nonconforming behavior. On the basis of such assumptions, the researchers thought customers would be more likely to report a shoplifting event when the thief was male rather than female, that female customers would be more likely to report an incident than male customers, that customers would be more likely to report an event when the shoplifter appeared as a hippie rather than a business professional. Only the third supposition was confirmed in this study.[68]

Three accomplices took part in the staged event; one was the fake thief, the other two were supposed store employees. The main task of the first store employee was to make himself readily available should the subject wish to report the incident. As soon as the shoplifter moved away to another location (after the theft), the first employee moved to the immediate vicinity of the subject and acted as though he was arranging merchandise on the shelves. He remained for a brief period. If the subjected reported the event then it was called a "high" willingness to report. The second fake store employee acted more directly and vigorously in order to increase the likelihood of reporting. He asked the subject for assistance in identifying a possible shoplifter in two different ways. If the subject reported the incident in these cases it was termed a "medium high" or a "medium low" willingness to report. All subjects who did not report went into a "low" willingness to report category. Subjects totaled 212 people, of which 191 were adults, 21 were students. Overall 62 subjects (29.2 percent) were rated high, 73 (34.4 percent) were medium high, 28 (13.2 percent) were medium low, 49 (23.1 percent) were rated low. Among just the adults those four figures were, respectively, 31.9 percent, 37.2 percent, 13.1 percent, 17.8 percent. All variations of cases in which the thief appeared as a hippie were reported more frequently than all variations in which the thief was straight. That is, it didn't matter whether the hippie was male or female, or whether the customer was male or female, the hippie was always more likely to be turned in. Steffensmeier and Terry stated, "A hippie identity or label constitutes for many subjects in this research, a master status, a pivotal category, or a central trait, which greatly increases the individual's vulnerability to stigmatization as a deviant." In general they found most subjects appeared to be inclined to not report the shoplifting incident and to avoid getting involved. In reporting the hippie shoplifter, some subjects "were very excited — even enthusiastic. When it was a straight thief many subjects hesitated, or thought twice — often resulting in no report." The researchers concluded that "the imputation of deviance resides not only in the fact of deviance per se; it also depends heavily on the meanings that the audience attach to the behavior and the actor. Willingness to report deviant acts can be assumed to depend on the deviant's other social identities, a significant clue to identify being provided by his appearance."[69]

Another study investigated the reporting of a clearly observed theft as a function of the race and sex of the thief and the sex of the observer. Location of the experiment was in a college bookstore with a subject between a pretend employee and a pretend thief. Shoplifters were black and white, male and female. A total of 240 white male and female shoppers (all between 18 and 30 years of age, and presumed to be students) were given the opportunity either to spontaneously report an act of shoplifting or to confirm the fact that the theft had occurred by responding affirmatively to a direct question. After the theft, when the thief had moved to another part of the store, (in the spontaneous condition) the store employee approached the subject and said, "May I help you?" In the confirmation condition the clerk said, "Did you see that guy (girl) steal that book?" For the 240 subjects in the spontaneous condition just 6.7 percent reported the theft, with 10 percent reporting a black male thief, 6.7 percent a black female lifter, 3.3 percent a white male, and 6.7 percent a white female pilferer. For the 111 female subjects, the four reporting rates were, respectively: 9.9 percent, 18.2 percent, 3.4 percent, 6.7 percent. For the 129 male subjects the number were: 5.3 percent, zero percent, 3.2 percent, 6.7 percent. In the confirmation condition the 113 subjects reported the theft 51.3 percent of the time. Within that category the 51 female subjects reported the incident 52.9 percent of the time, with 55.6 percent reporting a black male; 57.1 percent a black female, 61.5 percent a white male, and 40 percent a white female shoplifter. For the 62 male subjects the five numbers were, respectively, 50 percent, 58.8 percent, 66.7 percent, 37.5 percent, and 35.7 percent.[70]

Overall researchers concluded there was a nonsignificant trend for blacks to be reported more than whites and that thefts perpetrated by blacks were confirmed significantly more often than thefts by whites. Promptings, and so forth, significantly increased the frequency of theft reports. "This increase seems to have been due to the fact that it is easier to ignore an event than to lie when asked a direct question about the event," they concluded. They also declared that clearly observed acts of shoplifting were not spontaneously reported by the majority of shoppers. Those extremely low report rates (relative to other studies) they obtained may have been a function, they felt, of two factors. One was the relative unpopularity of the establishment being stolen from. The second factor was the potential "costs" of reporting. Another conclusion drawn was that acts of shoplifting were reported at a higher rate when the observer had reason to believe that the theft had also been observed by an employee. That confirmation rate was still not overwhelming and was done with "some degree of hesitancy." Shoplifters were not reported and/or confirmed differentially as a function of their gender, but female shoppers tended to report thefts more frequently than did males.[71]

In a 1977 study, college students staged shoplifting events in Laramie, Wyoming, and in the Southern California communities of Pomona and Long Beach. As in the other studies the object was to determine which shoppers would report the thefts. One of their assumptions was that the degree of ambiguity involved in an emergency situation often determined whether a bystander would intervene. A bystander was more likely to help if the action required was clear — if the situation was unambiguous. Those staged events were blatant, in front of 262 shoppers, 103 male and 159 female. Twenty-eight percent of shoppers in Laramie reported the shoplifter, 16 percent in California; 25 percent of male shoppers in Wyoming reported the thefts, just seven percent in California; 31 percent of female shoppers reported in Laramie, 21 percent in California. Thirty-five percent of Wyoming shoppers over 30 reported the pilfering, 16.6 percent in California; 17 percent of Wyoming shoppers under 30 reported, 16.6 percent in California. To remove any ambiguity the researchers installed prominent antishoplifting signs in Laramie, explaining the action a shopper should take if he saw a shoplifting event. Seventeen percent of all shoppers under 30 reported the theft before the signs were displayed, 41 percent afterward; 35 percent of all shoppers over 30 reported the event before the signs, 22 percent afterwards; for male shoppers it was 25 percent before, 35 percent afterwards; for female shoppers the respective numbers were 31 percent before and 22 percent afterwards. Since the signs encouraged the reporting of shoplifting by younger shoppers the researchers felt the signs did indeed remove ambiguity. However, the same signs decreased reporting by older shoppers, which caused the experimenters to speculate that the signs may have made too strong a demand on older shoppers to react in a specific way, resulting in their rejecting the demand — a psychological reaction.[72]

Personality makeup of shoplifters was also studied. One effort looked at 32 people charged with shoplifting (20 female, 12 males, aged 12 to 68; 56.3 percent were under 30, but a greater proportion of males, 66.3 percent, were under 30 than females, 50 percent) and referred to a psychiatric medical facility in Ottawa, Canada, for assessment, between 1971 and 1975. In their opening comments the researchers quoted a Judge Jean Sohier who estimated the number of thieves who stole from department stores in the Brussels-Liege area of Belgium was, over a period of five years, approximately one tenth of the total adult population. They declared that two percent of sales were lost to shoplifters and passed on to consumers as a two percent sales markup; that in the United States in 1973 merchants lost $16 billion to shoplifting, vandalism and employee dishonesty; that in 1974 that amount was $20 billion. After studying the 32 referrals the researchers concluded that the three factors leading to a shoplifting act by "unusual shoplifters" were one extrinsic factor, namely the sales technique, and two intrinsic factors, a passive-aggressive personality, and a stressful interpersonal situation. The latter acted as the precipitating event, a crisis that the shoplifter could not resolve by any other more appropriate means. They found no evidence of kleptomania. Their "unusual shoplifter" category included those whose shoplifting was not seemingly motivated by a need or a desire for the goods and whose personal history suggested shoplifting was an outlet for underlying stress or dissatisfaction.[73]

Researchers from a Southeastern university tested subjects using a personality test, the MMPI. In their initial subject pool were 154 subjects: 83 male, 71 female. From the screening it was determined that 39 males and 13 females reported they had shoplifted many times; 13 males and 10 females said they had pilfered once; 31 males and 48 females stated they had never stolen. Sixty subjects were then selected and given the MMPI. Their intention was to look at the interaction between personality and shoplifting behavior. They first categorized what they felt were the different views of the shoplifter: one was that he had a normal personality and shoplifted because of environmental temptations, another was that the thief had a normal or neurotic personality and shoplifted to cope with acute anxiety and depression. A third view, the psychiatric, presented shoplifting as behavior resulting from depression caused by conflict during the first three stages of psychosexual development. A fourth view was that shoplifting was indicative of a delinquent or criminal personality. Upon analyzing their data, the researchers concluded that the hypothesis that shoplifting was performed by delinquent/criminal personality types was supported by the psychopathic classification of the profiles of chronic shoplifters while the hypothesis that suggested depression caused pilfering was supported only for female one-time offenders. The idea that the behavior was the result of situational environmental stimuli rather than personality factors, they declared to be not supported. Shoplifting behavior, they concluded, was "considered symptomatic of general maladjustment ... it was determined that individuals who shoplifted only once were classified as neurotic. Their shoplifting behavior was interpreted as an overt act indicating poor coping skills and a covert call for adjustment assistance. Chronic shoplifters were classified as maladjusted with psychopathic tendencies.... The chronic shoplifter's personality was described as hostile, deceitful, emotionally shallow, impulsive with delinquent tendencies and high energy levels."[74]

Also studied this decade were the attitudes of people toward shoplifting. A 1978 poll of students at the State University College in Plattsburgh, New York, show that students thought shoplifting was wrong to do themselves, but okay for others to do, except their own children. More than half said they had shoplifted at least once in their lives, although only 17 percent had shoplifted in the past two years. Seventy-five percent said that if they spotted a lifter while working in a store they would turn him in, but less than 25 percent would turn in a pilferer otherwise. Those students indicated that the most effective deterrent to shoplifting was television cameras, while the least effective were signs threatening prosecution and guards at the door.[75]

During October 1976, a consumer survey on shoplifting was conducted in three shopping centers in Omaha, Nebraska. It produced 1,141 useable questionnaires. Asked how many of 100 customers on a given day shoplifted, the survey's median response was 7.86 — close to the New York study which had found one in 12 pilfering. Estimates of the extent of shoplifting given by the respondents produced higher numbers for females, for younger age groups, for lower educational levels, and for lower income levels. Researcher Leonard Prestwich speculated that there may have been a relationship between estimates of the extent of shoplifting and actual involvement in the activity. Of the 1,126 who answered the question whether or not shoplifting resulted in any cost and/or inconvenience to the respondent as a customer, 91.4 percent said yes. Of the 1,029 who said yes, 96 percent listed a cost or inconvenience. Thus, at least 87.7 percent (96 percent of 91.4 percent) were aware of a cost or inconvenience. Among those who listed a cost or inconvenience, 91.2 percent listed higher prices. When respondents were asked what they would do if they saw someone shoplifting, the responses were as follows: tell someone in authority, 69.3 percent; tell them to return it, 3.5 percent; stare disapprovingly, 1.9 percent; physically stop them, 1.3 percent (these totaled 76 percent, called by the researcher an antishoplifting attitude); do nothing, 20.8 percent; laugh, ask for half, etc., 0.4 percent (a total of 21.2 percent, not antishoplifting); others and "don't know" totaled 2.8 percent.[76]

Another study had 77 undergraduate students from a large southern university watch videotaped scenes depicting rule-breaking (shoplifting) and non-rule-breaking (non-shoplifting) behaviors of an actress portraying a "hippie" and more mainstream woman. The research studied how people who monitored television cameras in retail establishments made decisions about whether or not certain actions of shoppers were "reportable." A basic psychological premise was that appearance was indicative of identity and subsequently was the basis of observed differential audience reactions. A conclusion drawn from the study was that when the actress was dressed as a hippie the audience felt she would have been less personally affected by being convicted for shoplifting than when she was dressed straight.[77]

Researchers in the 1970s studied in depth the factors involved in the decision to prosecute or release apprehended shoplifters. Lawrence Cohen and Rodney Stark looked at the cases of 371 shoplifters apprehended at a large metropolitan department store located in California. It had five full-time store detectives (two white, one black, and two Mexican-Americans) and supplemented them with five part-time detectives during the holiday season. Cohen and Stark pointed out that under labeling theory, blacks were more likely than whites to be labeled criminal or delinquent and the lower classes more so than the middle classes, regardless of their actual behavior. It was in that sense, they felt, that it became meaningful to suggest that persons in penal institutions were mainly "political" prisoners. Cited were two older studies from the pre–1960 era which reported a significant racial bias in the treatment of shoplifters—blacks were disproportionately apprehended which, it was suggested, stemmed from differential surveillance behavior, and they were also disproportionately turned over to the police rather than being released after they were apprehended. In the store under examination by Cohen and Stark it was the policy never to act on suspicion, but to act only when the detective had personally observed a theft. That was, they thought, perhaps responsible for the fact that fewer persons were apprehended than one might have expected, given a staff of five detectives: "Indeed, one must wonder whether the store wouldn't be money ahead if it employed no detectives and simply wrote off shoplifting losses." When apprehended, a suspect was asked to sign a form confession, which also constituted agreement not to sue for false arrest. Store policy made referral to police mandatory under any of five conditions: 1) the suspect used violence to resist arrest; 2) if the suspect threatened to sue; 3) when the suspect had a prior record for shoplifting; 4) when an adult arrested could produce no identification; 5) when a suspect refused to be searched, refused to sign the confession form, or would not provide the information necessary for the case history. Under other circumstances, referral to police was at the discretion of the store staff.[78]

Researchers who spent many weeks watching the detectives work observed that virtually everyone apprehended was ashamed, remorseful, and cooperative. Tears were many times more common than defiance. While the store checked out each suspect with a private security company that maintained records on all shoplifting apprehensions in all member stores in the region, rarely did they have a person with a prior shoplifting apprehension — only three in the course of a year. That caused the researchers to conclude that "it seems that virtually no one continues shoplifting after being apprehended once." In total that year, 54 percent of the 371 people apprehended were released. By race, 47 whites were nabbed (53 percent released); 190 blacks (56 percent); 116 Mexican-Americans (50 percent); 18 others (61 percent). Of the 202 juveniles caught, 65 percent were released; 169 adults (41 percent); 192 males (55 percent); 179 females (54 percent). By occupation, 203 students were detailed, (54 percent released); 24 housewives, (52 percent); 24 skilled workers, (54 percent); 39 unskilled workers, (56 percent); 81 unemployed, (28 percent released). People who stole goods worth less than $30 numbered 293, (62 percent released); 78 people stole goods worth more than $30, (26 percent released). While blacks made up 51 percent of the apprehended, they were 22 percent of all shoppers; whites were 13 percent of those detained, but 46 percent of the shoppers; Mexican-Americans were 31 percent of detainees, 25 percent of shoppers. Those arrested by the sole black full-time store detective were 75 percent black. Concluded the researchers, "the shoplifter's age, sex, and race are found to be unrelated to his subsequent release or prosecution. Social class is also found to be insignificantly related to shoplifting disposition, except for the high rate of prosecution of the unemployed. On the other hand, the value of merchandise stolen is found to exert a strong independent influence upon the release or prosecution of apprehended shoplifters." They added that "these data simply contradict the notion of racism in the handling of offenders. They also largely contradict the premise that deviance is in the eye of the beholder. What people do seems to be more critical." Not emphasized by the study leaders was the fact that the two groups which comprised 47 percent of the shoppers contributed 82 percent of all detainees. Since at least one study, cited earlier herein, found no difference by race for baseline shoplifting rates it may also be true that, at first, what people are seems to be critical in drawing surveillance in the first place.[79]

A study led by Michael Hindelang examined the records of shoplifters apprehended by drug and grocery stores in Southern California in 1963, 1965, and 1968. Overall, he concluded that the decisions of stores to refer detainees to the police were found to be more closely related to the value of the goods stolen, as well as to what was stolen and how it was stolen, than to the characteristics of the offender. Four variables were investigated in the study: age, sex, race, and total retail value of the items stolen. The mean value of items stolen per incident in 1963, 1965 and 1968 were, respectively, $3.06, $3.31, and $3.39. Median values were $1.27, $1.35, and $1.39. For all years any suspects who had stolen items worth $1.90 or more were classified as large value cases. Totaling all three years, 6,261 cases were studied, 3,406 small value cases with a referral rate to police of 13 percent, 2,855 large value cases of which 40 percent were referred to the police. The referral rate for the 4,555 whites was 25 percent; 28 percent for the 1,706 non-whites; of the 2,943 female detainees, 25 percent were referred, 26 percent of the 3,318 males. By age the referral rate was 21 percent for suspects 17 and younger (2,362), 31 percent for 18 to 29 year olds (1,569), 26 percent of 30 to 39 year olds (830), 24 percent for the 40-plus suspects (1,500). Generally, the referral rates went up across the board for the three selected years. For example, referral rates for the 1,596 suspects in 1963 were 23 percent, 24 percent for the 1,931 cases in 1965, and 28 percent for the 2,734 suspects in 1968. Rates for females, for the three years were, respectively, 22 percent, 25 percent, 28 percent; for whites, 22 percent, 25 percent, 27 percent; for 30 to 39 year olds, 22 percent, 30 percent, 37 percent. Because of the large increase in referral rates to the police for high value shoplifting cases, Hindelang noted that it meant that even if the number of shoplifters apprehended had stayed the same from 1963 to 1968, a crime wave would have been generated by an apparent change in the behavior of stores. One thousand apprehended shoplifters in the large value category at the 1963 referral rate would have resulted in 340 offenders becoming known to the police, while 1,000 detainees in the same category at the 1968 referral rate would have resulted in 450 perpetrators known to the police — a rate increase of 32 percent. Hindelang concluded that, overall, when the retail value of the items stolen was controlled, the age, sex, and race of the shoplifter were not related or were only slightly related to the probability of being referred to the police. His results were different from those of Cameron, he speculated, because she had not controlled for the value of items stolen, which may have made a difference. Cameron studied shoplifters apprehended by the private security force of a Chicago department store between 1943 and 1949 and found that 10 percent of the females (but 35 percent of the males) and 11 percent of the non-blacks (but 58 percent of the blacks) were referred to the police for prosecution.[80]

A study by Erhard Blankenburg based on German data looked at some of the same issues. In his report's background, he cited an earlier German study involving 220 vocational school students, 15 to 18 years of age, who belonged to the lower social strata. Thirty-nine percent of them admitted they had shoplifted before, 12 percent said three or more times. Of the 89 who admitted shoplifting, only four had been known to the police. Experimenters staged 40 shoplifting events in a Freiberg, Germany, supermarket. Thirty-nine of these events went undetected; one was aborted by the experimenter on the belief he was being watched too closely. Department store managers in that country estimated that about 10 percent of all shoplifters were detected. From that assumption Blankenburg concluded that the definition of salesperson did not include behavior necessary to detect offenders. A good salesperson was characterized by polite and helpful behavior; a true detective, however, had to be suspicious and not preoccupied with helping. "The behavior of salesperson and detective are inconsistent," he said. In the first three months of 1966, German department stores failed to report 67 percent of offenders; in the same period of 1967 only 30 percent were not reported. However, during the latter period a "zero" tolerance had supposedly been implemented. When Blankenburg investigated almost 400 cases of shoplifting from a Freiberg store he found that eight percent of those nabbed were foreigners, but they were 15 percent of those who received a sanction for the offense. He found that the greater tendency to report foreigners was independent of the value of the object stolen. Age also was found to have an effect, with the young and the old less likely to be sanctioned; also, blue-collar workers were punished more often than white-collar employees. In the 6 to 13 age group were 7 percent of those nabbed (they were 10 percent of the general population); 4 percent were reported to the police, zero percent were sanctioned. For the 14 to 17 age group those apprehended were 12 percent (6 percent); 9 percent reported, 10 percent sanctioned. In the 18 to 24 group were 13 percent of apprehensions (15 percent of the population); 14 percent reported, 14 percent punished. Those 25 to 64 years old comprised 56 percent of those apprehended (56 percent of the population); 65 percent of those were reported, 68 percent were sanctioned. The group 65 and over totaled 12 percent of detainees (13 percent of the population); 8 percent of those were reported and 8 percent sanctioned.[81]

After reviewing the factors that determined the probability that shoplifting would be detected, reported, and sanctioned Blankenburg concluded that within the context of a low detection rate of 10 percent or less, enforcement was highly selective and customers appeared unwilling to report even flagrant cases. Even when German retailers had an announced and publicized policy of 100 percent reporting and prosecution, only 70 percent of the detected offenders were reported, and only 55 percent were sanctioned. Stores, police, and courts generally, he decided, "look the other way in most cases, and they initiate formal prosecution very selectively.... Detection itself is selective, because detectives follow a 'strategy of success-oriented suspicion.'" He then cited Cameron's work in which she determined that store detectives singled out persons with "big bags or wide coats, or blacks." All strategies of suspicion exhibit some kind of selectivity, he observed. Even if stores declared vehemently that all detained offenders would be prosecuted, he added, "there are still economic reasons not to invoke court procedures.... Thus, there are very good reasons for the victims of shoplifting not to invoke the criminal process."[82]

Another study investigated what effect being apprehended for shoplifting had on subsequent shoplifting behavior. Questionnaires were given to students at four high schools in small communities in the Pacific Northwest. A total of 1,189 useable surveys were obtained. From that data, 751 youths (63 percent) self-reported they had shoplifted at some time in their lives, 50 percent by the time they were 10 years old, 39 percent between the age of 10 and their last school year, and 26 percent during their last school year. Pilfering was slightly more prevalent among males (68 percent) than females (57 percent) and among the lower class (66 percent) than middle class youths (57 percent). Of the youths who had shoplifted, 25 percent (189) reported being apprehended by store personnel at least once; 17 percent (127) reported being caught at least once by their parents. Study leader Lloyd Klemke found that youths who had been apprehended for pilfering reported more subsequent shoplifting than those who went unapprehended. Youths exposed to police contact during apprehension reported more subsequent shoplifting than those who were handled by store personnel alone. Also, apprehended youths reported a stronger deviant self-concept and less fear of store antishoplifting devices. Klemke concluded that labeling theory explained his findings, at least in part.[83]

Researcher Richard Lundman also looked at shoplifter referral rates on the basis of race, age, and gender. He looked at the security records of the midwestern branch of a nationwide department store chain, a total of 664 cases, over the period 1973 to 1975. Lundman concluded that a substantial proportion of the variation in referral rates was attributable to the retail value of the item stolen. Without taking retail value into consideration, the data indicated that non-white, older and, to a lesser extent, male apprehended shoplifters were referred to the police more frequently than their white, younger, and female counterparts. When the cases were controlled for retail value, race still played a consistent but diminished role. Even with the effects of retail value as a control, the study declared that "race continues to play an important role in the referral decision." With regard to gender, the effect washed out when controlled for retail cost. However, age played a consistent and important role in the referral decisions, even with retail value controlled. Those 18 and over were referred to the police more than those under that age. Concluded Lundman, the data "suggest that the retail value of the item stolen, the age and the race of the shoplifter, all relate to the decision to refer to the police. The sex of the offender, however, appears to be unrelated to the referral decision."[84]

When Dean Rojek looked at apprehension records, he did so from a sociological perspective, one that included the idea that police reports had come to be seen as statistics reflecting the social control of crime. Therefore, any analysis of official statistics had to take into consideration not only the offender but those who defined the behavior as criminal. The growth of a private police industry had by then led to an industry which contained more private than public police. Commented Rojek, "The private law enforcement sector is plagued with ill-qualified personnel, who are grossly ignorant of the law or the powers of arrest, and are virtually unregulated." He looked at data from 12 retail stores in a midwestern city, outlets that were matched in pairs, based on gross receipts, floor space, number of staff, type of goods sold, and so forth. Then the stores were put in one of three categories: 1) discount; 2) medium-priced department stores; 3) high-priced department stores. Researchers looked at shoplifting apprehension records for the 12 stores over a two-year period, at the number of arrests, and sex and age of the offender. Rojek found a marked variation in the total number of apprehensions, as well as in the percentage distribution by age on the matched pairs of stores. Also, he found what appeared to be a progressive decline in the number of apprehensions as one moved from the low- priced to the high-priced stores, as well as something of a shift from older to younger offenders. For example, for the six stores (three matched pairs) in category one the number of apprehensions ranged from a low of 178 to a high of 696. In the other six stores (from categories two and three) the variation was from 84 to 197; there was only one case of overlap. In the first six outlets the percentage of offenders aged 17 and under ranged from 34.6 percent to 56.8 percent; in the other six it was 32 percent to 70.7 percent. The percentage range for offenders aged 46 and over, in category one, ranged from 3.5 percent to 20.5 percent; in the six outlets in categories two and three, that range was from 1.2 percent to 7.2 percent with, again, only one instance of overlap.[85]

Rojek declared that the data was found to differ significantly between matched pairs of stores by age and in half of the cases by gender. The frequency of arrests, along with the age and sex of the alleged offenders were seen to fluctuate with "almost wild abandon" from store to store. It all seemed to suggest that varying police tactics and varying reactions to the problem of shoplifting produced almost totally unrelated results. The only meaningful finding was that the shoplifting rate was not greater for females than for males and that "in all stores a pervasive sense of concealment and specialization tends to shield security personnel from company rules and regulations, thereby ensuring them of a significant degree of autonomy." Considering the question of who became an official statistic and why, he wrote that "the private police statistics utilized in this study stand as a prominent example of differential law enforcement, with shoplifting rates gathered from one source bearing little relationship to the distribution from another source."[86]

During the 1970s, youth was firmly established as the principal offender with the percentage of detainees under 30 regularly being approximately 75 percent. Whether it was because they did in fact steal more, or because they were easier to spot and apprehend, or because they were watched more than other groups, remained unclear. When a particular group was watched more closely than other groups because it was, or was believed, to produce shoplifers at a greater rate, then it could become a self-fulfilling prophecy. It was also a period of widely fluctuating numbers estimating losses due to shoplifting. Within a few years those numbers ranged from annual losses of $0.5 billion all the way up to $5 billion. In the end no one knew. Retail outlets continued to fight back in various ways. Yet it never seemed to do much good. The more money retailers spent on technology and security personnel the more shoplifting was portrayed in the media as increasing at an out-of-control rate. This panicked the retailers, some of whom spent even more money on supposed fixes, and so it went. Many studies were done in the 1970s on various aspects of the problem. Conclusions may have been difficult to draw but most could be seen as verifying the idea that apprehension and referral rates for the offense were in the hands of a private police power which often used that power in an erratic and differential way with regard to society's various groups.

Chapter 6

STORES SUE SHOPLIFTERS, 1980–1989

"Loss prevention can be profitable." — *Chain Store Age Executive*, 1988

"Shoplifters beware — Knogo is watching." — *Business Week*, 1986

During the 1980s, laws continued to be enacted which favored the retailers in their quest to reduce shoplifting. By early in that decade it was permissible in some states to detain the suspect once the merchandise had been concealed or the price tag altered; in others, the suspect had to leave the premises with the stolen goods before the apprehension could be made. Trade publication *Security Management* reported in 1983 that statutes which gave retailers immunity from their actions in detaining suspects, provided that detention was "reasonable," were reported to be on the books in each of the 50 states.[1]

Around the same time a Virginia law existed which gave merchants the right to stop and question shoppers who set off antishoplifting alarms. That law came into effect after lobbying by the Giant supermarket chain and other retailers. Giant was then pressing for similar legislation in Maryland and the District of Columbia.[2]

However, more important to retailers was the extension of laws allowing retailers to claim civil damages from shoplifters. Under a 1980 law in Oregon, a store owner could send a letter to the offender demanding he return the merchandise, an amount equal to the price of the stolen goods and an additional amount to cover the costs of the procedure. Merchants could request actual damages up to $500 from adults and up to $250 from minors. If a person refused to pay, the retailer could take the offender to small claims court. In the case of children, parents were liable for the amounts. Criminal prosecution could be instituted separately but many store owners reportedly dropped the criminal shoplifting charges when the offender agreed to pay the civil fine. One man was arrested in an Oregon store for taking a bottle of cologne worth $15. The store sent him a letter demanding $115 — the cost of the item and a $100 fine. Spokesmen for large retail stores said that most people agreed to pay the fines, "but some times grudgingly." By the time the law was one year old, the store had sent 1,100 letters, 600 of them to parents of juveniles. Ninety percent of the parents were said to have responded by paying the money demanded.[3]

By 1988, 30 states had responded by enacting laws designed to provide civil remedies for retailers. Every state that had a civil recovery law for shoplifting held adult offenders liable for paying the damages and penalties allowed by the civil recovery statute. Fifteen states with such laws declared that parents or legal guardians of juvenile shoplifters were responsible for paying damages and penalties. Most such laws applied only to businesses. Several types of damages could be awarded, depending on the state — damages for the value of the stolen merchandise, actual, and punitive and exemplary. The amount of damages that could be requested varied by state. Some statues allowed a retailer to request only the difference between the full retail value of the item before the theft, and its value when recovered. Actual damages were commonly allowed by civil recovery laws and were defined as the amount a retailer actually lost as a result of a shoplifting incident. Examples were: cost of damages to other goods, the cost of arresting a shoplifter (wages of investigators, etc.), and so forth. In some states, retailers could also request penalty or exemplary damages; they were designed to compensate stores and to act as a deterrent. For example, some states allowed retailers to request three times their actual damages. After calculating the damages, a store sent the shoplifter a demand letter and a copy of the state's civil recoveries law. If no payment followed, a second letter was sent. If that produced no result, then the retailer took the matter to small claims court. For retailers with in-house recovery programs it was said they produced payment results in 40 to 50 percent of the cases. Many retailers opted for civil recoveries programs run by outside firms. Those programs were also said to produce a 40 to 50 percent recovery rate.[4]

In all cases, civil recovery could be used either as an alternative or in addition to traditional criminal prosecution. Newark, California–based Ross Stores had a 34 percent success rate over two years. They used an outside company — most of which charged 30 to 35 percent of the money collected from shoplifters. Commented David Whitney, corporate director of loss prevention for Ross, "Prosecution and civil recovery let people know that we are tough. Unfortunately, I have a feeling that civil recovery will become an alternative to the criminal court system. It should be used as an enhancer. We have had good luck with it and people know we use it. Word gets out."[5]

Figures from a five-year study financed by the U.S. Law Enforcement Assistance Administration and released in 1980 declared that shoplifting cost a household in America $200 per year. This figure was said to be "double previous estimates of dollar losses" but still considered conservative because it referred to the cost of pilfered goods only, and not to the costs of shoplifting prevention.[6]

Hysteria surfaced once in a while, as it did in the trade publication *Drug Topics*, which asserted in 1981 that one out of every three small-business bankruptcies was due to shoplifting. Writer Dana Cassell introduced no evidence to support that statement.[7]

When the National Coalition to Prevent Shoplifting (NCPS) issued a report in 1981, it stated that shoplifting was the country's most expensive crime, accounting for monetary losses in excess of $16 billion. By comparison, United States bank robbery losses in 1979 were put at $47.5 million. Consumers paid for it all, through prices higher by five to seven percent on average. The group said that over 50 percent of shoplifting apprehensions were of people 13 to 19 years old while among student-age violators girls outnumbered boys by a ratio of four to one. A 1979–1980 survey of 3,550 retailers in 20 states, conducted by the same coalition, showed that 56.3 percent agreed with the statement that shoplifting "has definitely increased in the past two years." While more than 30 percent indicated they had problems with employee theft, more than 70 percent of the retailers indicated problems with shoplifting. Comparing the seriousness of the two crimes, 82.4 percent named shoplifting as the more serious crime. Also explored by this survey was who retailers thought was doing the shoplifting. More than 55 percent strongly agreed that females were more likely to shoplift than males; 63.6 percent strongly or somewhat agreed that teenagers were more prone to pilfering than adults. Over 46 percent strongly or somewhat agreed that racial minorities were more prone to shoplift than others were.[8]

Surveyed at the same time were 49,376 students in those 20 states. Almost half of those respondents, 47.6 percent, strongly agreed with the statement that retail clerks watched teenage shoppers more closely than they watched adults. Half of those students admitted to having pilfered. Six out of every seven students who admitted to shoplifting indicated they were not caught. Although 27 percent of students who pilfered planned to do so in advance of their entry into the store, almost 70 percent claimed they made their decision to steal in the store. However, 76.1 percent of the students who had shoplifted indicated they would not continue to do so in the future. Asked about their motivation for stealing, the students responded as follows: 35.15 percent said they didn't have the money to pay for the item; 26.61 percent did it for a thrill; 27.33 percent did it on a dare; 24.58 percent just acted on impulse; 9.01 percent did it to "get even" with retailers due to stores' higher prices.[9]

When the NCPS issued its 1980–1981 report, it put its estimate of total shoplifting losses at a sharply higher $24 billion, up from $16 billion for the previous year. That was said to represent a cost-per-household of $307 annually, up 42 percent over one year. The coalition went on to estimate losses at 6.6 percent of 1980 retail sales in the food, general merchandise, and drug store categories. That percentage was the median response from the 4,275 retail owners and managers who were surveyed and asked to estimate shoplifting costs, including the value of the goods lost, and the expense of security personnel, equipment and prosecution. Also, 100,671 students were queried with 49 percent of them admitting to the offense. Of that 49 percent, 30 percent said they would continue. Looking at the students who were caught, seven percent got as far as court, and five percent were sentenced or fined. In this survey, 71 percent of the retailers acknowledged a shoplifting problem; 74 percent stated that pilfering was a more serious problem for them than was employee theft.[10]

As in past decades shoplifting was viewed by many in the 1980s as rising dramatically. David Proper of the Golub Corporation of Syracuse, New York, which ran 60 supermarkets in the region, said the occurrence of the offense was on the rise. Coos Bay, Oregon, Police Sergeant Charles Knight said that, on a percentage basis, "shoplifting is one of our fastest growing crimes." Many were said to put the increase down to economic hard times while, wrote *U.S. News & World Report*, "others, however, trace the jump in stealing to what they see as a general breakdown in ethics."[11]

Contributing to the atmosphere were media reports which exaggerated and bordered on the hysterical. Atlanta, Georgia–based NCPS declared in 1982 that for every $100 retailers took in, they lost nearly $7 to pilferers. That would put the shrinkage rate at an incredible seven percent.[12]

Writing in a trade journal called *Volume Retail Merchandising* Ian Abramson said a few months later that "the most ignored, fastest growing, and hardest to control crime in the world today is shoplifting." He claimed that losses of that nature exceeded $26 billion a year in the United States alone. Then he went on to state that it would be absolutely impractical — if not impossible — to apprehend and prosecute even five percent of the perpetrators for public relations reasons and because the court and penal institutions were not equipped to handle the load. Somewhat surprisingly, Abramson then offered the opinion that the major contributors to the offence were the victims themselves: "One cannot turn on the TV, listen to the radio, or read a newspaper or magazine without being exposed to some form of advertising by merchants designed to create a desire or need for a variety of products. This works very well except that by creating an atmosphere for impulse buyers without adequate security, they're encouraging possible customers to indulge in 'impulse shoplifting.'" In his view, the only way to possibly control the situation was for retailers to spend more money on security personnel and product.[13]

A couple of months later, Abramson was back with a column in which he castigated retailers again. This time he argued there was a strong likelihood that stores had laid too many people off during hard economic times, forgetting that not only was staff a form of inventory control, but lack of customer service created frustration leading to new or first-time shoplifters. Also noted by the columnist was that internal theft, according to the National Retail Merchants Association (NRMA), was the leading cause of shrinkage, "but shoplifting activity has increased as the economy worsens." No evidence was cited by Abramson to support the latter contention.[14]

In an effort to determine more accurate shrinkage rates, the trade publication *Stores* sent out 1,000 questionnaires to retailers; 180 were returned. That was said to be a substantial response rate for that type of survey and, according to NRMA vice president Jay Scher, it "reflects the high level of interest in this area." Collectively the responding companies operated 10,629 stores in 1981, generating sales of $28.8 billion. Average shortage figure for the respondents for 1981 was 2.08 percent of total retail sales; 2.05 percent in 1980, and 2.08 percent in 1979. By industry segment, the range reported was fairly small, from a high of 2.31 percent shrinkage in women's ready-to-wear specialty chains to a low of two percent in junior department stores. In between were the mass merchandise chains, at 2.19 percent. Based on the 1981 figure from the U.S. Bureau of the Census that total retail sales of general merchandise, apparel, and jewelry amounted to more than $185 billion, *Stores* concluded that shrinkage among all United States retailers for 1981 amounted to more than $3.8 billion.[15]

Illustrating, once again, the use of exaggerated numbers was an article in the magazine *Aging* by Gary Feinberg. He argued that "in fact, shoplifting is the fastest growing form of larceny ... with losses amounting to over $24 billion annually." As a source, he cited a 1974 article, although Feinberg's article was published late in 1983. That cited article, which did use the $24 billion figure, itself gave no source for that figure.

When *Stores* came up with the $3.8 billion figure for shrinkage, mentioned above, it asked its respondents to estimate the percentage of the shortage caused by internal theft, external theft, and record keeping. Respondents laid almost equal blame: 33 percent, 32 percent, and 31 percent, respectively. That meant that annual shoplifting losses were in the neighborhood of $1.3 billion.[16]

Numbers used in media accounts varied tremendously. In the space of one 12 month period the figures were all over the map. *Forbes* magazine stated that shoplifting added up to an estimated $7 billion to $9 billion in nationwide losses. *Time* reported that the total for shoplifting in a year could go as high as $8 billion. Pinkerton retail security specialist Peter Haas said that pilferage, up 10 percent from the previous year, then totaled $3.6 billion, or 1.8 percent of all retail sales. Finally, Lindsay Brown, writing in *USA Today,* declared the annual loss attributed to shoplifting was $2 billion. According to Haas the typical shoplifter was a white female between the ages of 23 and 43. It was those people who did the most shoplifting. On the other hand Brown, who also worked in retail security, cited the number of apprehensions in one store in San Jose in one year. Among those 477 apprehensions were 25 male adults, 43 female adults, 155 male juveniles and 254 female juveniles. He did note that "security personnel possibly observe females more because statistics indicate them to be more prevalent shoplifters (a self-fulfilling prophecy)." Nevertheless, Brown went on to conclude, based on the above numbers, that the majority of shoplifters were juveniles (approximately five-to-one) and female (about two-to-one).[17]

When the Retail Council of Canada released its shrinkage survey of Canadian retailers it put the percentage as ranging anywhere from one to five percent of sales, with an annual dollar cost of $1.5 billion. Half of the companies reporting indicated shrinkage levels between 0.75 percent and 1.99 percent; a further 25 percent of firms reported shrinkage of two percent or more. The median for all companies was 1.36 percent.[18]

Taking the number exaggeration to even greater heights was the British business publication *The Economist* which stated, without supporting details, in May 1986 that "some put the cost of shoplifting at $50 billion a year to American retailers alone." Nor was any mention made of who those "some" were.[19]

In *Journal of Retailing*, Warren French and his coauthors dealt with the problem in hysterical tones, stating that retail losses from shoplifting were assuming "epidemic proportions" with estimates of losses from shoplifting ranging "up to $31 billion annually, depending upon what elements are included as shoplifting costs." Another $100 million per year was spent on equipment designed to prevent or detect shoplifting, and these costs, said French, had been cited as a prime cause in one-third of all small business bankruptcies. Just as disturbing for him as the dollar cost of the offence was the increase in the incidence of this crime — "at least 300 percent in the 1970s alone." Again, no data supported that contention. Yet the apprehension rate, he claimed, was "less than 3 percent." The nonprofit National Coalition Against Shoplifters (NCAS), operating under a grant from the U.S. Department of Justice, had tabulated data received in a questionnaire from 670 retailers in 21 states. Twenty-seven percent of those retailers said they had a problem with employee theft, 73 percent with shoplifting; 85 percent of those retailers said shoplifting was the bigger problem. Retailers who felt there had been a definite increase in shoplifting in the past two years numbered 87 percent. They reported a shrinkage rate of 6.6 percent, although they were told to include other costs such as the cost of security and of prosecution. It may have been such exaggerated writing that prompted Alexanders, a New York City department store, to prohibit, in 1983, unaccompanied minors from entering its store altogether.[20]

When the Retail Council of Canada released the results of another shrinkage survey, they reported it had declined to 1.28 percent of total sales in 1988, down from 1.36 percent in 1985. About 25 percent of the responding companies reported shrinkage of 0.75 percent or less, while another 25 percent reported a rate of 2.0 or more. Those retailers attributed 50 percent of the shrinkage loss to customers, 25 percent to employee theft, and 25 percent to bookkeeping and paperwork errors. While the Council reported a declining rate of shrinkage, they reported it amounted to $2 million a day in 1988, up from $1 million a day in 1985, without explaining the seeming discrepancy. Said Mel Fruitman, vice president of the Retail Council, "Can you imagine what an uproar there would be in the media if every day of the year there were an armored car holdup or similar type of theft of over $2-million a day? That is the amount that Canadian customers (and employees) regularly steal from our stores." Actually, using their figures, the loss to customers and employees was $1.5 million a day, the other $0.5 million went to paperwork error.[21]

In a more reasoned and analytical article, Douglas Espinosa noted that shoplifting statistics reflected a more equal demographic breakdown in terms of offenders. And they also indicated that the type of clientele a store attracted directly related to the type of shoplifter it would encounter. For example, if patrons were mostly female then the store would encounter mostly female shoplifters. If patrons were mostly older males, naturally the store would encounter more older male offenders. In a two-year period for three different hardware chains, 87 percent of those apprehended were male, 13 percent female. Four percent were juveniles, eight percent were 18 to 29 years old, 43 percent were 30 to 49, 45 percent were over 50 years of age. Fully 25 percent of all those apprehended were 65 to 80. Minorities made up just three percent of those caught. Generally, updated surveys indicated shoplifters were 55 percent male, 45 percent female; 16 percent were under 18; 34.5 percent were 18 to 29; 49.1 percent were 30 years and older. That caused Espinosa to wonder if older people were becoming shoplifters for the first time and if males were shoplifting more than they were 10 to 20 years earlier. He concluded both of those outcomes were unlikely, that "new training materials and increased open-mindedness have taught security professionals to be more cognizant of those whom they might not have suspected before. In short, today they suspect everyone."[22]

A survey by accounting firm Ernst & Young said United States retailers lost about $20 billion a year to shrinkage. This report put the number at 1.84 percent of sales in 1988, 1.83 percent in 1987. Still, they claimed there had been a 29 percent jump from the level in 1982 through 1986. Of those surveyed, 41 percent said they believed that theft in their stores was drug-related, 14 percent said it was not drug-related, and the rest didn't know. By that time, 21 percent of United States merchants had adopted drug-testing techniques for their employees.[23]

The number of shoplifting thefts known to the police in the United States was 688,494 in 1979, 744,049 in 1980, 741,800 in 1981, 775,065 in 1982, 804,051 in 1983, 766,920 in 1984, 903,242 in 1985, 1,023,447 in 1986, 1,027,322 in 1987, 982,555 in 1988, and 1,059,765 in 1989. Yet in annual self-report data collected from a large national sample of high school seniors there was virtually no change in shoplifting activity between 1977 and 1988; 30.2 percent reported in 1977 that they had shoplifted during the past year, 30.4 percent in 1988. At no time between 1977 and 1988 was there more than a four point fluctuation in the percentage reporting recent shoplifting activity, whereas FBI data showed about a 300 percent increase in shoplifting since 1973. It caused researcher Lloyd Klemke to conclude, "Therefore, the increase shown in FBI data is more likely to be a product of changes in apprehension and reporting practices than a real increase in shoplifting behavior."[24]

Psychological explanations and morality tales were a regular feature in articles on the offence. One such article appeared in *Seventeen* magazine wherein Bill Davidson reported on a reformed teen shoplifter who changed after her arrest. Having been apprehended three times she was crying out to be caught. Her parents were divorced, her mother was away at work a lot, the girl wanted to be accepted at high school, and so on. In large letters the article subhead read, "Kathy seems like an average sixteen-year-old. But she's one of over five million teens across the country who walked off with thirteen billion dollars worth of merchandise last year. This is her story...." Not only is the $13 billion a highly exaggerated number, but that is the amount attributed just to teenagers. In the closing paragraph, Davidson said that "with Kathy now seemingly under control all we have to worry about is the estimated five million other teen girls who shoplift." Over the course of the article what had been five million shoplifting teenagers had suddenly become five million pilfering teenage girls.[25]

Texas developed the Shoplifter Offender Program which, among other things, featured hours of talk therapy. Gary Solomon and Joseph Ray constructed a 20-item Shoplifters Irrational Beliefs Scale, which they administered to the program's 94 participants, 76 percent of whom were female. They found the three most frequently endorsed irrational beliefs of shoplifters were, in order: 1) If I am careful and smart, I will not get caught; 2) Even if I do get caught, I will not be turned in and prosecuted; 3) Even if I am prosecuted, the punishment will not be severe. Solomon and Gay found those beliefs to be routinely endorsed by the majority of participants in the Offender Program, prior to group attendance. Other items on the scale had to do with things like merchants deserving what they got, everybody did it so it was okay for me, etc. Yet, all three top beliefs were based on fact and reality; none of them were irrational.[26]

Good Housekeeping unrolled a weepy, feel-good saga in July 1986 with a title that harked back to the 1950s—"I was a shoplifter." It was the tale of a suburban mother of 30 with two children, a husband with a good job, and so forth. One day she was arrested for shoplifting a piece of costume jewelry. Tearfully she offered to pay for the item but the manager said no; his store had a prosecute-all policy. Taken to the police station the woman was photographed, fingerprinted, booked, and released that day. That evening she told her husband (who worked long hours) that she had been stealing for years: "I showed Don bags and bags of articles—clothing, cosmetics, jewelry—that I had stolen over the years and hidden in our big storage closet." Although the word kleptomania was not mentioned, the language of that concept was used: "My shoplifting was beyond my control—I just couldn't stop myself, any more than I could explain it." Her lawyer suggested counseling. At first she said no but later relented and enrolled in therapy. The judge agreed to release her if she entered a community rehabilitation program. She did. Then she took night-school courses and began to work toward a degree. She ended the story by enthusing, "And I'll never shoplift again — because I'm happy with me."[27]

Ladies Home Journal published the same type of story, except it was about women in general. First though, it was necessary to exaggerate the numbers to make it appear that adult women made up a substantial portion of the pilferers. With no supporting data, reporter L. B. Taylor, Jr. claimed that between 25 percent and 33 percent of all shoplifters were women between 20 and 50; that it was often called "the housewife's crime." While those statements may have been true at one time, they had not been for many decades. Taylor went on to say that an estimated 140 million instances of pilfering occurred in stores each year (attributed to unnamed "experts") but only about four million of the offenders were caught. He put shoplifting totals at $2 to $5 billion per year, a crime that cost each United States household $200 each year. It caused him to wonder what accounted for this upsurge in shoplifting. He wondered why well-off women stole. Experts believed, he told us, that most female shoplifters carried the habit over from their teenage days. For some women, pilfering provided an emotional outlet, an escape from monotony, depression, or even neglect. Doctors Michael Geurts and Everette Johnston of the University of Hawaii were cited as saying that shoplifters often had problems such as obesity or an unhappy social life, and that shoplifting provided a unique gratification for them. Reaching way back into the past, Taylor remarked that in some cases pilfering appeared to be associated with unsatisfied sexual desires. According to Dr. Abe Fenster, chairman of the psychology department at New York's John Jay College of Criminal Justice, "Often women tend to steal frivolous luxury items, the sort of thing they might receive from a lover." Taylor added, "They may even experience some psychical satisfaction from the act itself." Other unnamed experts were cited who thought that the anti-establishment attitude fostered in the 1960s had contributed to this "rip off authority" belief, particularly among women then in their late 20s to early 40s. He seemed to be suggesting some kind of delayed reaction for that 60s attitude to settle in, but it was all unclear. Other points Taylor mentioned were that most women who stole didn't consider it a serious crime and were shocked to learn that it was a form of larceny. They believed that if they were caught they could rectify the situation by paying for the goods, or they would get off simply with a lecture. "That may have been true years ago," warned Taylor, "but today most merchants prosecute shoplifters."[28]

In Canada, reporter Alan Hustak stated that psychiatrists suspected the majority of shoplifters "unconsciously want to be caught." Edmonton, Alberta, psychiatrist John Hamilton Brooks attempted to establish a self-help group — similar to Alcoholics Anonymous — to help shoplifters to help themselves. He placed an ad in the local daily, the *Edmonton Journal*, inviting shoplifters to attend group therapy sessions. However, he withdrew the offer after the Alberta College of Physicians and Surgeons threatened to reprimand him. According to Registrar Leroy Leriche, "We don't believe doctors should solicit patients, directly or indirectly" and, he added, "Dr. Hamilton Brooks is no better at treating shoplifters than anybody else." Brooks said that one-third of those who pilfered did so for gain. He was convinced the other two-thirds were emotionally ill, suffering from problems that could be diagnosed. Brooks believed that fewer than 10 percent could be classified as kleptomaniacs. Most of the shoplifters Brooks had treated were women who wanted more attention from their husbands or families: "Many want to be caught so they can communicate." Others, he thought, were basically suicidal.[29]

It was also a time when more and more frequently high-profile people turned out to be shoplifters. In Quebec, a popular government minister, Claude Charron, Government House Leader in the Parti Quebecois provincial party, was charged with stealing a $120 jacket from Eaton's department store. He was wearing it under his overcoat. Outside the store he ran from the security staff and finally had to be tackled. Charron resigned from the cabinet and was fined $300 in municipal court.[30]

Sue Bolich, Minnesota's representative in the 1988 Miss USA pageant had to step down because she had been caught shoplifting. Jolene Stavrakis took her place, but just for three days. Pageant officials discovered that two years earlier she had been arrested for the same offence. Reporter Louise Bernikow commented, "This kind of theft — typically a woman's crime, stemming from needs not necessarily financial, nor particularly rational — isn't new. But it is on the rise." Bernikow thought there was a new breed of shoplifter emerging: "She's young, has a good salary, money in the bank, and cash and credit cards in her purse." Yet women "would still be acting out problems of the female psyche in stores through female objects like clothes, jewelry and makeup — the most frequently lifted items."[31]

Bess Myerson, a former Miss America and television personality, was arrested in May 1988 when she was 64 years old for pilfering items worth $44.07 from a department store in South Williamsport, Pennsylvania. It caused *Life* magazine to grossly exaggerate shoplifting totals and the characteristics of the typical perpetrator. The magazine put retailer shoplifting losses for a year in a range between $8 billion and $50 billion and stated that "women steal more often than men. Most shoplifters are between the ages of 25 and 45." In trendy areas of Hollywood and Beverly Hills, it was reported that retailers regularly added the cost of observed shoplifted items to the bills of the thieves and sent them on to husbands and boyfriends for payment. Some of those pilferers were said to be famous.[32]

Ms. magazine then did a sympathetic feature on older women shoplifters, featuring Myerson. Among the excuses trotted out were low self-esteem, a hard period in one's life, feelings of intense loss, deprivation, and so on. "We know for a fact that more women steal than men," concluded the article. In reality, no such fact was known.[33]

Commercial Service Systems released their seventeenth annual survey of shoplifting in 1980. Data was obtained from 746 supermarkets owned by 12 companies, 125 drug stores owned by three firms, and 46 discount stores owned by four companies. It represented a total of 20,111 cases apprehended in 1979. The portion of shoplifters apprehended who were in the 12 to 17 age group was 26.7 percent (they were 10 percent of the general population); 18 to 29 year olds were 33.7 percent of those caught (21.7 percent); 30 to 39 year olds were 12.8 percent (13.7 percent); 40 to 49 year olds were 7 percent (10.3 percent); 50 to 59 year olds were 5.4 percent (10.5 percent); and 60 and over were 7.1 percent of those caught, but were 15.4 percent of the general population. There was next to no variation in day of the week and, as usual, the period from 3:00 to 6:00 P.M. was the clear winner in terms of the time of day that apprehensions most frequently took place. Data for the supermarkets alone indicated that January, February and March were the favorite months; October, November, and December were favorites for drug stores, but no clear favorites were indicated for the discount outlets. Supermarkets provided a total of 14,656 cases, of which males were 55.3 percent and females were 43.6 percent. The remaining cases were not identified by gender. The average number of items recovered per case was 3.1, with an average value of $7.37. Males pilfered an average of 2.5 items worth $6.49 while females took 3.8 items worth $8.47; adults stole 3.3 items ($8.61) compared to juveniles who took 2.6 items ($4.73). Overall supermarkets booked 30.8 percent of those apprehended and released the other 69.2 percent; males and females were booked about equally. Adults were booked 34.1 percent of the time, juveniles 24.7 percent. For drug stores only (4,015 cases—2,120 males, 1,849 females) the average theft was 2.6 items worth $9.67. Males stole 2.1 items ($7.57), females took 3.2 items ($10.76); adults took 2.4 items ($10.85), juveniles stole 2.7 articles worth $6.97. Drug stores booked 28 percent of those apprehended and released the other 72 percent. However, they booked a higher proportion of females (32.1 percent) than males (24.4 percent). Adults were booked 36.7 percent of the time, juveniles 18.4 percent. In the case of the discount stores (1,440 cases—736 male, 695 female) the average theft was costlier and a higher proportion of shoplifters were sent on to the authorities. Average number of items taken from a discount store was 4.5 with an average value of $25.44. Males stole 3.6 articles with a value of $22.34; females pilfered 5.6 items worth $28.29. Adults took 5.1 items ($28.65) while juveniles stole 3.4 articles with a value of $19.42. Those discount outlets booked 54.9 percent of those apprehended, releasing the other 45.1 percent. Of the males apprehended 49.7 percent were booked, 60.3 percent of the females; 63.4 percent of the adults were referred on to the police, 39.7 percent of the juveniles. Thus, the data showed that more males were apprehended as shoplifters than females. However, in all three types of stores women stole on average more items than did men, and the average value of items lifted was higher for the apprehended women. In all types of stores adults stole more items worth more money than did juveniles. Females were referred over to the police at a somewhat higher rate than were the males, perhaps as a result of stealing goods with a higher average value.[34]

Two years later Commercial Service Systems released its nineteenth annual report, based on apprehension data made in 911 stores. Around 92 percent of the data was supplied by stores in Southern California. As was usual with these surveys there was almost no difference in terms of favorite month of the year or favorite day of the week for shoplifting apprehension. Data was obtained from 668 supermarkets, 151 drug stores, and 92 discount stores. The average number of items pilfered per apprehension and the value of those goods for the three types of stores were, respectively, 3.2 items, $10.06; 2.5 items, $11.77; and 3.6 items, $29.11. Consistent with past surveys taken by the same firm, 65 percent or more of those apprehended were under 30, males outnumber females slightly among both adults and juveniles, and 3:00 to 6:00 P.M. was the favorite time of day, by a wide margin, for apprehensions. Percentage of lifters referred to the police ranged from a low of 17.1 percent for juveniles caught in drug stores up to 52.7 percent for adults apprehended in discount stores. To estimate the total shoplifting losses in United States supermarkets in 1981, this survey company multiplied the average supermarket theft, $10.06, times eight (estimated number of incidents per store per day) times 363 (number of operating days per year) times 34,900 (number of supermarkets in America) to arrive at a total of $1.02 billion. For 1981 there were 14,286 cases from 668 supermarkets for an average of 21.4 per store (16.6 in 1980); 6,810 cases from the 151 drug stores for an average of 45.1 (36.6 in 1980); 6,103 cases from the 92 discount stores for an average of 66.3 (26.2 in 1980). What looked like a huge increase in shoplifting events, especially in discount stores, was due to something else, as the article itself noted. A retailer with an aggressive apprehension program was, for the first time, part of the survey. As reporter Roger Griffin said of the data, "Shoplifting statistics reflect many variables, for example, the number of hours spent by one store on apprehension. Since we only know the end result and not the amount of time or the quality of the effort expended to obtain that result, we cannot, with certainty, calculate an increase or decrease in shoplifting in general."[35]

When Commercial Service Systems released its twenty-first annual survey of shoplifting, it estimated the United States supermarket industry lost more than $1.25 billion to shoplifters in 1983. The study was based on 31,081 apprehensions; 19,733 cases reported by 740 supermarkets; 3,997 cases from 150 drug stores; 7,311 from 111 discount stores. Sixty-five percent of those apprehended were under 30; 82.5 percent were under 40. The 18 to 29 age group made up 22 percent of the United States population yet comprised 38 percent of all apprehensions. Children under 12 and adults over 60 were caught only one-third as often as those groups' sizes would indicate. People in the 12 to 17 group were caught twice as often as their group size, 50- to 59-year-olds only half as often; 30- to 39-year-olds slightly more often and 40- to 49-year-olds slightly less often. Of those apprehended 55 percent were male, 45 percent female; 54 percent of adults caught were male, 46 percent female; 57 percent of juvenile detainees were male, 43 percent female. Adult females stole more items from supermarkets than males, 4.0 items to 2.7. Reporter Roger Griffin noted that estimating with certainty the extent that shoplifting alone contributed to total shrinkage was impossible. Commenting on the great range in percentage of shoplifters referred to the police, Griffin said, "The difference in policy regarding how many shoplifters are prosecuted does not appear to affect the number of apprehensions from year to year."[36]

Retailers continued to fight back against pilferers in various ways. One of the main ways was in the increased use of attaching sensitized tags to articles. It was called electronic article surveillance, or EAS for short in the trade. Those tags had been on the market since Arthur Minasy, chairman of Knogo Corporation, sold the first radio-frequency tag, developed in 1966 in his garage. Those so-called hard tags sold for $1 each; soft tags cost 25 cents each. As journalist Francesca Lunzer quipped, instead of spying of their customers, retailers now increasingly spied on their merchandise.[37]

Industry leader in the sensitized tag industry was Sensormatic Electronics Corporation who began marketing the invention in 1968, but did not make a profit until 1973, when it earned $191,000, or five percent after taxes, on sales of $3.8 million. In fiscal year 1979, the company earned $4.4

million on sales of $27.6 million. The National Retail Merchants Association (NRMA) estimated about 0.6 percent of total retail sales was spent on security measures to curtail shoplifting. Sensormatic estimated that for the average specialty store with one exit to guard and $1 million in annual sales, a single system and 10,000 tags would cost about $13,000. In the early days Sensormatic was too successful — it caught too many. Those first, early tags were designed to be hidden on the article. In one instance at a military PX, Sensormatic caught the commanding officer's wife before the first week was over. The company was quickly thrown off the base. After that, and similar events, Sensormatic learned that its customers—the stores— did not want to catch their customers shoplifting. They wanted merely to deter them from pilfering. Thus, the big, easy-to-see tag was developed. Regardless of how diplomatic the approach was to a customer who triggered an alarm, some innocent customers who had been asked to show receipts successfully sued retailers for false arrest. As a result, after industry lobbying, Georgia and a few other states passed laws making the sounding of an alarm grounds for a store to request a receipt from any customer who caused the alarm to sound. At the start of 1980, Sensormatic had 70 percent of the United States market for shoplifter security systems and over 50 percent of the European market. By then it had placed 13,000 systems. Number two in the industry and main competitor was Knogo Corporation with revenue in fiscal year 1979 totalling $11.2 million. That Long Island, New York–based firm had placed 4,000 systems since 1966. Third place in the industry was held by Checkpoint Systems, with $5 million in revenue in 1978. Its technology employed low-frequency radio waves and the company regularly attacked Sensormatic's microwave system as a potential hazard for customers.[38]

The industry expanded rapidly. For the year ending May 31, 1982, Sensormatic had revenues of $67 million, up from $7.7 million in the year ending in May 1977. Over that same period, earnings increased 400 percent to $15 million. Knogo had sales of $14 million in 1981 while Checkpoint had revenue of $10 million. According to Sensormatic, 96.4 percent of United States department stores, 90 percent of women's dress and specialty shops, and 98.2 percent of discount and variety stores had yet to install any kind of electronic security system. The company had hoped to move into supermarkets, at least to a limited extent by this time, but it had not happened. They could not afford to put tags on low cost items, such as cans of vegetables.[39]

By 1983 a Sensormatic system cost an average department store $35,000. The company then had 75 of the 100 largest department store chains as customers. It claimed that the use of its system allowed a retailer to reduce shoplifting by as much as 70 percent. Sensormatic had finally gained a few supermarkets as customers with about 350 SensorGate systems installed in 35 stores. Company president Ronald Assaf claimed that losses in those food outlets had dropped by 50 to 60 percent. Grocers attached the magnetically sensitive tags to only their high-priced items. At the checkout stand the clerk put purchases right into bags; the customer exited through the gate to pick up his bags. The gate cost about $4,000 to buy, or $100 a month to lease; an average United States supermarket needed about 10 gates. Sensitive labels cost around 3 cents each, with about 15 person-hours a week needed to apply them to articles.[40]

While on the one hand some retailers were content with the large labels, others wanted smaller labels. A drawback with the large tags was that they were more expensive and could only be attached to large, pricey soft goods. Knogo announced in the mid 1980s that it had invented the Electro Thread, a two-inch long strand of wire that was easy to conceal but hard to remove. It cost about one cent, if purchased in bulk, and could be attached to a variety of goods. Rather than being removed by clerks it was a tag that was simply deactivated.[41]

By 1986 the theft protection industry generated an estimated $200 million in revenue per year. Sensormatic led the way at $89 million, Knogo was next at $36 million and Checkpoint remained third with $27 million. Checkpoint's system was a radio frequency-based product while the other two companies used microwave technology. Three types of tags then were in use. One was the reusable hard tag which was removed by a clerk. However, it was a technology becoming obsolete. A second type was a disposable tag that was electronically deactivated, but left on the item. Third was a soft tag that was also electronically deactivated but more sophisticated since it could be integrated with price-marking and scanning equipment.[42]

As reporter S. Caggiano noted, however, all was not perfect in the EAS industry. Over the years a reputation for false alarms and mediocre reliability had made EAS devices less than enthusiastically received. Tags could be shielded or detuned. False alarms could be generated from such sources as hearing-aid batteries, sudden changes in atmospheric conditions, and electronic key rings. In the newer systems, the low frequency negated the problem of detuning by body fluids. Savvy shoplifters could no longer place the tag against their bodies or under their arms to defeat the system. All EAS systems, wrote Caggiano, reduced shrinkage initially due to the deterrence aspect of the system. However, the duration of maximum effectiveness depended on the performance reliability and integrity of the EAS system used and the degree to which other loss prevention measures were used simultaneously. Caggiano thought that easily defeated systems without other simultaneous loss prevention programs would see a shrink-age resurgence in as little as six months.[43]

In the ladies room at Washington, D.C.'s fashionable Woodward & Lothrop department store, toilets used to routinely clog up as a result of shoplifters' attempts to flush away the familiar white plastic anti-theft tag. In Chicago, some people sold $100 shielded shopping bags to safely trans-port garments with anti-theft tags past detection gates. Sensormatic — with fiscal year 1988 sales of $123 million — was then test marketing TellTag. If someone tampered with it, the tag sent a signal to store secu-rity. Walk a TellTag past a detection gate and it started beeping by itself. Each existing hard tag contained a piece of metal or some other material that functioned as a radio receiver and transmitter. Detection gates broad-cast radio signals which were picked up and reflected by the tag, thereby tripping an alarm. They cost about $1 each; TellTag was priced at $4 each.[44]

Giant company supermarkets did an average of $400,000 in sales per week, in the mid 1980s. Those outlets, which had installed EAS systems, felt they had eliminated 90 percent of shoplifting and that their profit mar-gins had improved an average of 0.5 percent. With less uniformed secu-rity guards needed, outlets believed they were saving about $17,000 to $18,000 per year. A Sensormatic system cost $4,000 to $5,000 per check-out lane, installed, with maintenance running about $100 per lane per year. A Checkpoint system cost $3,000 to $4,000 per lane, plus $200 instal-lation. Maintenance was about $200 annually per lane. Typically a super-market used 4,000 to 7,000 detection strips per week with their cost being in the range of 3 cents to 3.5 cents for either system.[45]

At Old West, a chain of casual clothing stores, shrinkage used to be one to two percent of sales. After the installation of an EAS system it was said to have dropped to 0.3 percent. Company vice president Peter Doniger said something about shoplifting which no one else had mentioned: "secu-rity officers are aware of special codes shoplifters use to inform one another if a particular store is a good target for shoplifting. For example, the code may consist of small colored marks. Red may mean a store is not a target for shoplifting and green may mean the store is a good target." Likely it was all an urban myth.[46]

Other methods to curtail shoplifting were also tried. Subliminal mes-sages were said to be used in greater numbers. One distributor estimated that the number of stores using them in 1986 was 1,000, with 100 percent growth in one year. They were audio messages played through the store's sound system: customers consciously heard only piped-in music, but sub-consciously they supposedly heard another message that was being played at a frequency below conscious perception — a message linked to shoplifting prevention. Larry Roberts, a distributor of such systems, suspected that subliminal messages also had an effect as well on employee theft. Roberts claimed his retail customers experienced shoplifting reductions ranging from 3 to 80 percent. David Riccio of the Viaticus Group (a subliminal tape manufacturer) reported his clients saw consistent reductions in shoplifting of 20 to 40 percent. While standard off-the-rack tapes were available, Roberts recommended that tapes be custom-made to a store's demographics, since terminology, accents, and speech patterns varied across the country.[47]

With fairly regular hype about dramatic increases in shoplifting there was always somebody trying to market some new type of prevention device. One was Denver mannequin repairman Jerry Gutierrez who, as the 1980s ended, planned to market Anne Droid with a video camera in her eye and a microphone up her nose, to catch pilferers in the act. Nothing more was heard of Anne Droid. Sensormatic then was producing a closed-circuit surveillance system that allowed store managers to watch cashiers on one side of a split screen and cash register receipts on the other. Some stores hid their cameras behind smoked-glass ceiling domes. A number of upscale chains like Chicago's Marshall Field placed store detectives in hollow, eight-foot columns with two-way mirrors, known as Trojan Horses. By this account at least a dozen major retailers broadcast barely audible subliminal messages over the outlet's audio systems. The sounds ranged from police sirens and clanging jail-cell doors to muffled sentences such as "Stealing is dishonest." A company called Color Tag sold a tag with a dye-filled capsule that exploded if it was removed incorrectly, leaving non-removable stains on the item and on the thief's hands. A few years earlier the Marshall Field chain removed tags from 90 percent of its merchandise. At the same time it set up a comprehensive program to train employees how to spot shoplifters. As well, it started to hold managers accountable for losses. The retailer even offered a $500 reward for tips that led to pilfering employees. Reportedly, stealing dropped by 33 percent.[48]

Underlying it all, though, were the stereotypes and preconceived notions of store security personnel. Researcher Vincent Sacco investigated the suitability of crime prevention through mass media approaches as techniques for the management of the problem of retail theft. Two major communication strategies were identified. The first used antishoplifting messages which were addressed to the potential offender while the second involved the attempt to indirectly deter shoplifting by increasing public awareness, reportability, and informal social control. In summary background data, Sacco looked at one study which analyzed private police data from matched sets of retail stores, concluding that due to differing security procedures, the frequency of arrests, and the age and sex of offenders were seen to fluctuate with almost "wild abandon" from store to store. Similarly, a different study which involved interviews with and an examination of the shoplifting files of security personnel in nine stores in northeast Scotland found that the security personnel's pre-existing stereotypes of "typical" offenders affected the likelihood of apprehension. Of particular regard, in that respect, was the stereotype of the unaccompanied lower class juvenile. As one researcher commented, "the more variable the rate of detection and the more discretionary the decision to prosecute, the more will criminal statistics reflect administrative rather than criminal behavior. Sacco concluded that "a major commitment of human, financial and other resources to large-scale anti-shoplifting media campaigns is probably not justified at this time."[49]

According to a study by accounting firm Arthur Young the average loss prevention budget for retailers was 0.32 percent of sales in 1982, 0.34 percent in 1986, and 0.35 percent in 1987.[50]

Just who was responsible for what part of total shrinkage continued to draw some attention although, as in the past, other media mostly attributed the entire loss to shoplifters after, in many cases, drastically inflating the shrinkage total in the first place. A 1982 study of retailers and their dealing with shoplifters found that those stores who were the most successful in controlling the problem attributed at least half their losses to employees. Retailers with lesser records of success fingered shoplifting as the main factor. Some executives blamed paperwork for shortages; short-shipping by venders was also considered a factor.[51]

That same year the NRMA estimated that shoplifters caused only 30 percent of its members' losses, employee theft contributed 40 percent, and "other" was responsible for the remaining 30 percent.[52]

Typical of the differing viewpoints was a statement by Gary Rejebian, a spokesman for the Illinois Retail Merchants Association, who said, "Shoplifting causes the greatest losses for a retailer." That same *Time* magazine article went on to declare that the biggest group of criminals, "say the experts, are store employees." Also cited was a study by the Arthur Young firm, which determined that employees accounted for 44 percent of shrinkage while shoplifters were responsible for 30 percent.[53]

Peter Haas, a retail security specialist for the Pinkerton firm conceded that employees were a major contributor to losses: "they steal almost twice as much as your customers." If a retailer employed a lot of teenaged clerks then, said Haas, "you are most probably a victim of sweetheart checking. This age group is notorious for this type of retail theft." In this type of theft the clerk worked with the customer to charge him less than the purchase price.[54]

A 1989 report said that shrinkage in the United States had increased 29 percent over the previous five years, amounting to $1.8 billion, and slightly over 2 percent of gross sales. Regarding apprehended thieves, 89 percent were customers, 11 percent were employees. Of the customers caught, 52 percent were male, 57 percent were 18 or older. Apprehended employees were 54 percent female, 75 percent were 18 years old and over.[55]

Researcher Lloyd Klemke determined that experts from three different national organizations estimated that shrinkage losses could be attributed to the following: 40 to 50 percent due to employee theft, 25 to 30 percent due to shoplifting, and 15 to 30 percent to accounting errors.[56]

Things were much the same in Canada where the Retail Council of Canada said that shoplifting represented about 20 to 40 percent of most stores' shrinkage, with the average being about 30 percent. The group noted that the number of arrests for the offense had risen dramatically over the past few years, due not just to the fact that more people were stealing, but also to the fact that more stores were getting tougher, arresting and prosecuting more of those caught shoplifting. Despite that, declared the Council, it had not changed the relative importance of shoplifting in relation to shrinkage totals: "it remains constant at about 30%."[57]

In the UK, according to a study done by Stirling University, shrinkage amounted to about one percent of retail sales, equaling around 1.5 billion pounds Sterling a year, and was rising at the rate of 15 percent annually. Retailers said that paperwork errors accounted for between 15 percent and 25 percent of the total losses. But that "administrative theft" was said to be declining as accounting systems became more sophisticated. Also noted were sales staff "who steal at least as much as the customers do."[58]

As in the past, the 1980s saw many academic studies done on the issue. A questionnaire survey of 1,800 high school students in New Brunswick, Canada, found that the number of students who had shoplifted at least once was 53.9 percent. Of the shoplifters 53.3 percent were male, 46.7 percent were female. At the same time a questionnaire completed by 530 respondents at three major shopping malls in that area determined that 64.6 percent of those respondents said they would not report a shoplifting they had witnessed.[59]

When researcher Lloyd Klemke gave a self-report questionnaire to 1,189 nonmetropolitan high school students at four high schools in the Pacific Northwest, his results indicated that 751 (63 percent) of the respondents reported that they had shoplifted sometime in their life. Among those students who had ever shoplifted, the study revealed that 30 percent of male shoplifters, compared to 20 percent of the female shoplifters, reported being apprehended by store personnel. Klemke also looked at the percentages of adolescents shoplifting items of different dollar value since school had started that school year — almost nine months before the questionnaire was given. In the category taking items valued under $2, 73.7 percent of males replied never (over those nine months), 11.6 had taken one such item, 7.4 percent 2–4 such items, 3.0 percent 5–10 items, 5.3 percent 11-plus items. For females 80.6 percent said never and the other percentages were, respectively, 8.5 percent, 5.7 percent, 1.6 percent, 3.6 percent. In the category, taken items valued between $2 and $10 the respective percentages for males were, 86.4 percent, 5.1 percent, 4.1 percent, 1.4 percent, 3.0 percent; for females the respective numbers were; 89.8 percent, 4.8 percent, 2.6 percent, 1.4 percent, 1.4 percent. In the final category, taken items valued over $10, 93.7 percent of the male student respondents said never, the other figures were, respectively; 2.8 percent, 1.6 percent, 0.2 percent, 1.7 percent. For the female students, the numbers were 96.4 percent, 1.2 percent, 1.2 percent, 0.2 percent, and 1.0 percent.[60]

George Washington University undertook a study to examine what effect, if any, the use of antishoplifting measures had on consumers' attitudes toward a store. The study was conducted in Washington, D.C., where 52 shoppers were interviewed upon leaving stores. Paying for the report was PSA International, a trade association of companies who specialized in the design, installation, and servicing of closed-circuit television systems. Attitudes reflected essentially white collar, middle and upper-middle class values. Of those surveyed, 73 percent believed shoplifting losses were significant. However, the vast majority stated they were not affected by any store's use of anti-shoplifting measures. Ninety-five percent agreed that the use of those measures was not an invasion of privacy. In fact, said the study, "most shoppers seem almost oblivious to the use of antishoplifting techniques." While smaller retailers were said to have embraced closed-circuit television monitoring systems larger retailers were said to have shown greater reluctance to use electronic surveillance, "apparently fearing that negative customer reaction might show itself in lower sales."[61]

Steven Thurber and Mark Snow conducted a study in a retail supermarket in a Pacific Northwest community to determine the effects of warning signs on shoplifting behavior. Research was conducted across four consecutive periods of one week each. Cigarettes were picked as the target articles. Weeks one and four were the baseline periods while during weeks two and three antishoplifting signs were hung above the cigarette carton display. In week two the sign (specific) read "CIGARETTES are the items most often SHOPLIFTED in this store." In week three the sign (general) said "EVERYONE pays for SHOPLIFTING." Contrary to expectations, the antishoplifting signs were associated with increases in shoplifting rates when compared to baseline levels. Shoplifting frequencies were 372 (baseline, week one), 637 (specific sign, week two), 532 (general sign, week three), 376 (baseline, week four). Those differences were significant. The ratio of shoplifting frequency to sales remained fairly constant for the two baseline periods at three percent, but increased to five percent with the specific sign and four percent when the general sign was displayed. Thurber and Snow concluded that signs may have somehow prompted antisocial behavior.[62]

One staged shoplifting event compared type of dress and physical size of the thief. Two shoplifters were used. One was 5'6" tall and weighed 140 pounds while the second was 6' and 255 pounds. Each varied between being well-dressed and being poorly dressed. As each thief appeared in each condition 25 times there was a total of 100 staged thefts. Thirty-three witnesses reported the crime, 30 of them after the pilferer had left the store. The well-dressed shoplifter was reported twice as often as the poorly dressed one (22 to 11); the smaller thief was reported twice as often as the big one (22 to 11). Of the 33 people who reported the crime, 21 were more than 60 years old. The large poorly dressed man was reported two of 25 times, while the small well-dressed man was turned in 13 of 25 times. In each of the other two conditions (small and poorly dressed, large and well-dressed) the thief was reported nine of 25 times.[63]

Although millions of dollars was spent on security devices, those systems seemed to have a limited impact. Between 1979 and 1984, at a time when the use of security devices was rapidly increasing, shoplifting incidents were said to have increased by 14 percent. A research study by the Police Foundation — with funding from the National Institute of Justice — examined the power of arrest to deter shoplifting. Hubert Williams conducted the study in nine outlets of a department store chain in a large American city. Data was collected and analyzed for 1,593 cases recorded by the chain's security department. Two groups were assessed, those caught by store security and then arrested by the police, and those caught but released from the store without arrest or referral to police. Williams found that, shoplifters, as a group, who were arrested were neither more nor less likely to commit shoplifting offenses during the following six months than those who were apprehended but released from the store without being arrested. Also, both groups were arrested for subsequent crimes other than shoplifting at the same rate — about 10 percent for each group. Arrest did seem to have a significant deterrent effect on one group of pilferers — juveniles. Of those arrested for shoplifting, only four percent were rearrested for crimes other than shoplifting during the six month follow-up period. Of those juveniles released from stores without arrest, ten percent were later arrested for crimes other than shoplifting. Both groups were caught shoplifting again at about the same rate — six percent. Williams concluded, "For the entire group 10 percent of those apprehended and turned over to the police for arrest were arrested again within six months for shoplifting, while 9 percent of those apprehended but released without arrest were rearrested for a subsequent shoplifting offense."[64]

A Canadian study which presented 192 hypothetical cases to security officers at four different retail stores examined the decision to prosecute shoplifters. Seven different factors were presented in the cases: 1) cost of item stolen, high value ($20–$50) versus low value (under $5); 2) admission of the offense (yes/no); 3) sex of thief (male/female); 4) age of offender (young, 8–15; middle, 16–65; old, 66–80); 5) race (black/white); 6) attitude of thief (R&A: respectful and agreeable, versus D&D: disrespectful and disagreeable); 7) appearance (Good: neat, clean, and well-dressed, versus Bad: untidy, dirty, and poorly dressed). The results indicated that the value of the article stolen was the most important predictor in the decision to charge or release a suspect. Also highly associated with the decision to prosecute was admission of the offense. Researchers also found that the age of the suspect was significantly related to the investigators' decision making. When value of the item pilfered was controlled, age still related to prosecution. Security personnel told researchers of their folk knowledge of the anticipated response of the judiciary, in that cases involving the elderly were likely to be thrown out of court. Race was not found to be related to prosecution decisions. Researcher expectations that poorly dressed people were more likely to be charged were not met — in fact the reverse was true. Findings confirmed that the stolen item's value and the suspect's age were the most important predictors of the decision to invoke the law in response to shoplifting. Supported by the findings was the observation that extremes of the age range were associated with leniency. "In addition to these factors we identified two other factors associated with the decision to charge shoplifters, namely, the admission of the offense and the respectability of the suspect measured in terms of dress; well-dressed persons were more likely to be prosecuted than their poorly dressed counterparts. In addition, suspects who admitted to their offense were less likely to be charged than those who refused to do so, this being especially true for persons who were poorly dressed," noted the study. For example, in cases where a high value item was stolen, 46 were charged, 18 not charged; for low value articles the numbers were, respectively, 21 and 43. If the suspect gave an admission of guilt, 26 were charged, 38 not charged; if no admission was made, then 41 were charged, 23 not charged. In the case of young offenders, none were charged, 64 not charged, in the middle group 44 were charged, 20 not charged; for the elderly the respective numbers were 23 and 41. Forty well-dressed offenders were charged and 24 not charged, while 27 poorly dressed were charged, 37 not charged. In terms of interactions, when a well-dressed suspect admitted guilt, 18 were charged; 22 were charged when no admission was made. On the other hand, when a poorly dressed suspect admitted guilt, 8 were charged; 19 were charged when no admission was made. If the hypothetical thief was middle-aged and stole a high value item, then 31 were charged; 13 were charged for a low value article. Researchers concluded that while their findings generally supported the idea that "it is the characteristics of the act rather than the offender that appears to be most important, we also found that some offender characteristics are related to the decision to invoke the law."[65]

Another observation study of shoplifters studied 503 people randomly selected as they entered a small department store, part of a national chain, in a city in the southeast of England. In their background text, Abigail Buckle and David Farrington summarized several observational studies conducted in the 1970s. Those studies found that the percentage of randomly selected shoppers who stole something to be 8.4 percent (a New York department store — 6.4 percent of the males, 9.2 percent of the females); 5.2 percent (a second New York department store — 5.7 percent males, 5.3 percent females); 4.4 percent (Boston department store — 2.6 percent men, 5.4 percent women); 7.8 percent (Philadelphia department store — 6 percent males, 8.8 percent females); 0.8 percent (UK department stores — 1.9 percent men, 0.3 percent women); 2.0 percent (UK supermarkets — 2.3 percent men, 1.9 percent women); 5.5 percent (Dublin department and convenience stores — 4.4 percent males, 5.9 percent females). In Buckle and Farrington's study the store in question had a shrinkage rate of five percent. Results were that nine of the 503 observed customers (1.8 percent) took at least one item, four of the 142 males (2.8 percent) and five of the 361 females (1.4 percent). Most frequent offenders were those estimated to be over 55 years old (4.9 percent, compared to 1.0 percent of the remainder). None of the 24 juveniles shoplifted. Value of the items stolen was only 0.9 percent of the total value of the items taken out of the store by those customers — most purchased something. Assuming shrinkage at five percent, the total purchases (915.31 pounds Sterling) represented 95 percent of the stock and the corresponding value of the stock lost through shrinkage was therefore 48.17 pounds Sterling. The value of the items shoplifted (7.86 pounds Sterling) therefore, argued Buckle and Farrington, represented about 16 percent of stock shrinkage. They believed their estimate was on the same order as another researcher who had stated that 25 percent of stock loss was attributable to shoplifting, 35 percent to short deliveries, 25 percent to theft by employees, and 15 percent to shop-soiled goods. Because of this study, declared Buckle and Farrington, "we can be 95 percent certain that the shoplifting rate in the population is between 0.6 and 3.0 per cent." The researchers also suggested that the probability of any given shoplifting leading to apprehension and official police action was less than one percent and that "This study also suggests that the majority of stock shrinkage is not attributable to shoplifting, and that customers aged over 55 are especially likely to shoplift."[66]

Marking the 1980s was the pervasive use by retailers of electronic article surveillance systems—those ubiquitous tags to be found on items, the pricey ones to start with, but increasingly at all cost levels. Laws allowing retailers to sue shoplifters in civil actions for damages were enacted in a variety of states in the U.S., all designed to make life easier for the stores. Media numbers estimating the annual amount of shoplifting losses were exaggerated dramatically, allowing the media to concoct stories about the explosion of shoplifting, its epidemic status, and so forth. Usually those numbers had no basis in reality. Stock shrinkage stubbornly hung in at around the two percent level, as it had for decades. And most of that amount—roughly 66 percent of it—was lost due to causes other than shoplifting. Cases involving high profile offenders became a regular item in the media. Articles could still be found, almost always in female-oriented magazines, which analyzed the offence as predominantly a female problem—even to the extent of bringing back the old image of women achieving some sort of sexual satisfaction from shoplifting. To analyze the problem as female-oriented, these articles had to also fall back on very old images of shoplifters being mostly women. In fact, nothing had supported that concept for decades. What research was done indicated that shoplifters were fairly evenly divided according to gender.

• Chapter 7 •

PRIVATE JUSTICE SYSTEMS, 1990S

> "Customers should be outraged if a retailer is not practicing civil recovery!"—Read Hayes, security company executive, 1990
>
> "Shoplifting is really a lashing out."—*McCalls*, 1995

One of the biggest issues that revolved around shoplifting in the 1990s was civil recovery laws. Civil recovery was not a new concept—it was as old as common law. What was new were the civil demand laws being passed across the country. Those statutes made it easier administratively for merchants to collect for damages resulting from losses due to theft. Nevada in 1973 was the first state to enact a civil recovery statute. Prior to that, the legal damages retailers could recover for shoplifting offenses were small, if they were available at all. Two cases held the recovery laws to be constitutional. One was in Oregon Supreme Court in 1986 in which Payless Drug Store was suing the parents of a minor apprehended for shoplifting. The second was in 1987 in the Wisconsin Court of Appeals. All arguments including the amount demanded as well as the constitutionality of the demand were upheld. At the start of the 1990s, 35 states had civil recovery statutes.

In a criminal court, a retailer had to rely on the state to determine if he would receive restitution. However, as Read Hayes, vice president of a retail security firm, noted, "In a civil action, a retailer is in control of whom to demand restitution from through the civil demand process.... Criminal prosecution is a necessary evil. Although it is a good deterrent, sometimes the retailer is looked on as the 'bad guy.'" Criminal action was also a public issue. Because most arrest records were public records, anyone had access to them. Hayes argued that the high cost of security should be passed on to offenders, not to paying customers by way of higher prices. "Customers should be outraged if a retailer is not practicing civil recovery!" he exclaimed. Civil action in the form of demand letters was a private issue. Offenders were not fingerprinted, photographed, or incarcerated,

125

said Hayes, so the public did not have access to those records. Hayes explained, "All that is needed for civil action is a civil demand law in your state, a correct subject name and address, and a preponderance of evidence." In criminal action, proof had to be "beyond a reasonable doubt."[1]

Looking at such laws from a different perspective were researchers Melissa Davis, Richard Lundman and Ramiro Martinez, Jr., who declared that among the ways corporations used their enormous wealth was to support private justice systems complete with investigative, adjudicatory, and sentencing powers. Analysis revealed to them that retail value of the item taken, neighborhood social class, and physical resistance were among the factors determining private corporate justice for shoplifters in a civil recovery state. The findings suggested to them the part played by private justice systems in shaping public images of crime and criminals. Merchant privilege statutes, as they called them — giving retailers the right to reasonably detain, search, interrogate, and so on — "provide an excellent shield behind which the civil rights and personal dignity of suspected shoplifters may be abused with impunity.... Suspected shoplifters have been accosted and physically abused, handcuffed to a desk, slandered, or detained for an hour with immunity from tort liability being provided by the courts to the merchants in each instance." Civil recovery laws expanded those already extensive powers. They changed the financial costs of responding to shoplifting. In states with laws inviting large exemplary damages, catching pilferers could be a profitable activity for a store and its police. Within states with lesser exemplary damages, civil recovery reduced the costs. "In literally thousands of backroom store security and loss prevention offices, private store police determine the fate of those caught shoplifting. As has long been the case, some are released and others are arrested. Still others are now sentenced by private store police to civil recovery," they wrote.[2]

Davis and the others examined a department store in a major shopping mall in a large city. The store was one of 300 in the corporate chain. All 10 of the store's private police were part-time employees, paid $5 to $5.40 an hour. Those store police had extensive powers— the same powers and jurisdiction as given other police officers by state law, for example, the power to arrest. That store's private police were not constrained because the state Court of Appeals ruled that the "constitutional right against unreasonable searches and seizures does not ... render inadmissible evidence obtained by a private person without government participation, regardless of whether such evidence was obtained by a legal or illegal search." Also, store police were only partially constrained by Miranda with private store police freed (by an Appeals Court ruling) from strict guidelines provided that the interrogation was not protracted and, therefore, "clearly violative of the defendant's rights." Those merchant privilege statutes immunized the store police from criminal or civil liability for false arrest, false imprisonment, or unlawful detention, provided it was "reasonable." People suspected of shoplifting at this store were taken off the floor and into Loss Prevention where, explained the researchers, "They are searched. Their pockets, wallets, purses, and bags are emptied. Most are handcuffed. All are required to sit in a chair where a picture is taken of them and the shoplifted merchandise. The minority who physically resist are chained to the chair as well." Before the passage of a civil recovery law in that state in 1985, the store had only two ways of disposing of a suspect — release or arrest. This store's policy, prior to the civil recovery law, was to prosecute all shoplifters. Data was collected from the store for the years 1986, 1987, and 1988, with a total of 421 cases examined. Before October 1986, all suspects were arrested, with no exceptions. From that date until the end of 1988 arrests declined to 58.6 percent, with civil recovery instituted against the other 41.4 percent. Over those three years the store's private police recovered articles with a retail value of $29,471. Estimated wages for the 10 part timers was $41,015, thus there was a loss of $11,544. However, $7,500 in civil fines were paid to the store, reducing the loss to $4,044. As Davis observed, "Though civil recovery did not make catching shoplifters profitable at the store we studied, it did significantly reduce the cost."[3]

Civil recovery made perception of ability to pay a civil penalty an important determinant of disposition. Store police skimmed off the affluent for civil recovery and sent the less affluent off to the public criminal justice system. As compared to public police the private corporate police were much more proactive and intrusive. Those private police were also far less lenient. "Public police release most offenders in minor trouble with the law. The private corporate police we studied arrested nearly 60 percent of apprehended shoplifters even though most had taken items worth very little, almost all were entirely polite in their interaction, and very few resisted private police authority," commented the researchers. Davis, Lundman, and Martinez concluded that "private corporate justice systems are among the social control organizations shaping public images of crime.... Private corporate police are clearly among the agents of social control doing the screening. Just as clearly, private corporate police help create and sustain the link between social class and street crime by skimming the advantaged for civil recovery and sending larger numbers of poor people into the embrace of the public criminal justice system."[4]

New York retailers joined the group that could bypass criminal proceedings against shoplifters, granting them a clean record in exchange for reimbursement, on November 1, 1991. On that date a new civil recovery law came into effect, following the lead of 40 other states with similar legislation. Under it, a person caught shoplifting would pay a penalty not to exceed five times the amount of the stolen merchandise or up to $75, whichever was greater. For example, a retailer might demand a $75 payment on a $2 stolen magazine. Michigan had a similar law and a report there from the supermarket chain A&P said that 80 percent of people apprehended paid the requested damages and only five percent were caught shoplifting again.[5]

When New Jersey governor Jim Florio signed into law in August 1993 a measure that imposed civil liability on shoplifters who stole merchandise worth less than $500, New Jersey became the forty-fourth state to adopt a civil recovery act. As background, the *New York Times* cited Peter Berlin, executive director of Shoplifters Anonymous as saying that the offense had gone up pretty steadily since 1982, that one out of 11 people pilfer and that it cost $9 billion annually nationwide. Under the New Jersey measure the thief returned the item or paid full value if it was damaged and, in either case, paid a penalty of up to $150. Also, the offender had to pay court costs and lawyers' fees if a civil suit became necessary — that is, if a demand letter was ignored. Parents of minors were liable for those costs. Reporter Angela Delli Santi pointed out that some critics questioned the fairness of such a law since those who had the means to pay a civil penalty would be let go while those who didn't would be prosecuted. Other critics warned that if civil recovery were to replace the criminal justice system, incidents of shoplifting could actually increase. In New Jersey, a first time shoplifting offender could be fined up to $500 within the criminal justice system while a third time offender received a mandatory 30-day jail sentence and could be fined up to $1,000. Civil recovery laws were not intended for repeat offenders or for professional shoplifters. As originally drafted, the New Jersey bill would have forced retailers to choose whether to pursue a suspect criminally or civilly. However, the measure was amended on the recommendation of the state attorney general's office so that stores could seek civil or criminal prosecution, or both.[6]

Writing in the trade publication *Stores*, Michael Hartnett observed that retailers were moving cautiously to take advantage of the civil recovery option. Some had discovered that the use of the civil demand tactic could help them deter thefts while also helping them to defray the cost of loss prevention programs. A 1994 survey by the Security Research Project at the University of Florida found retailers used the option sparingly; civil demand was used in less than 25 percent of the shoplifting cases, and in only 15.3 percent of the cases involving employee theft — in both instances that was substantially less often than was the use of criminal prosecution. Project director and associate professor at the university, Richard Hollinger, said civil demand was used by no more than a third of the retail community. He added that department stores used civil demand in 25 percent of the cases for employee theft and 35 percent of the shoplifting cases. In discount stores, civil demand was used 30 percent of the time for employee theft and 33 percent for shoplifting. Some companies viewed it as a profit center, but it was also a logistic nightmare, which was why there was a growth in third party companies offering this service. The resulting complexity and confusion both held down overall use of civil demand and had fostered the growth of civil demand specialists providing outside services to retailers. The Children's Place, a 90-store chain that operated in 21 states, had used civil demand since 1989 and found it got the best response from a $150 demand above the cost of any goods involved. Carl W. Koberle, director of loss prevention for the firm, explained that civil demand was both a deterrent and a way of generating revenue. As to the decision whether or not to pursue a criminal or civil solution, he said that since each state had its laws structured differently he pursued a civil recovery in lieu of prosecution in some cases, but in others he pursued both. If he could apply both effectively, he did. Eckerd Drugs generated $1 million in annual revenue through civil demand, with a 55 percent rate of positive responses to its demand letters. It operated 1,700 stores in 13 states. The company prosecuted one percent of those it apprehended, based on whether the individual was a career criminal or was already listed in its shoplifting database. Said Lew Shealy, vice president of loss prevention for Eckerd, "Most of these people are our customers, and civil demand is user-friendly. If someone is spending $3,000 a year in prescriptions, you don't want to tell him not to come back in the store. It's better to charge him $200 in civil demand, knowing that person is not going to steal again."[7]

By mid–1996, civil recovery statutes had been enacted in 49 states and the District of Columbia. The sole exception, Delaware, was considering the implementation of such a measure.[8]

Audrey Aronsohn was an attorney with Simi Valley, California–based Civil Recovery Services, Inc., where she designed and implemented civil recovery programs for companies nationwide. She felt that civil recovery should not become a mechanism by which offenders could buy their way out of criminal charges. However, she noted that many company policies included waiving criminal charges for shoplifters if the offender assented to a trespass agreement — an affidavit assuring that he would not enter the store again. Under that type of agreement, if the person came back to the store, the charges could then elevate to burglary. Aronsohn argued that this often used tactic was ill-advised; the store was telling the thief not to steal from it again while tacitly encouraging him to steal from another shop. Instead, she argued, retailers should force a shoplifter to take responsibility in both criminal and civil court whenever possible. Another tactic she criticized was the immediate payment method whereby a retailer made his demand for civil recovery when the suspect was first detained by store personnel. A few states did prohibit companies from accepting cash from thieves when they were first detained rather than pursuing the matter through formal civil proceedings in court, but most states did not mention the issue. Allowing additional time between the theft and the demand for recovery would allow further review of the facts, reduce the chances of mistakes and, of course, resulting litigation; "Still more important, however, is the need to avoid the appearance of extortion." In 1999, Aronsohn wrote about the beginnings of a new trend in civil recovery wherein such statutes contained estoppel provisions. One example was a recent law enacted in Florida. The law included an estoppel provision that prevented a defendant from relitigating in a civil action the facts of a case in which he had already been pronounced guilty under the higher standards of the criminal law. In such cases, the perpetrator could not dispute his or her guilt, which had already been established by a higher court. The only issue was the amount of damages. Such laws and provisions, of course, made it still easier for retailers. The perils of having a too-harsh civil recovery program could be seen in an example cited by Aronsohn. In that case a jury ordered the Walt Disney Company to pay $65,000 for falsely accusing a patron of stealing a Mickey Mouse doll from a Disneyland store. In that case, under appeal in 1999 by Disney, the company's aggressive pursuit of cash payment for shoplifted items was found unreasonable. The accused was separated from her friend and questioned by security personnel. After she was interrogated for two hours, a security guard discovered a receipt for the presumed stolen item. An employee of Disneyland also verified that the customer bought the doll.[9]

In Canada, Zellers department store instituted its own loss recovery program in London, Ontario, in 1993, extending it across the country to the rest of its 310 outlets in 1995. The company sent a demand letter for $225 in damages to a Winnipeg woman whose 14-year-old son was caught stealing $59.95 worth of merchandise in May 1995. The mother paid the money but then decided that she should not be held responsible for her son's actions. She sued in small claims court for the return of the money but the court upheld the retailer. However, in 1996, Justice Gerald Jewers of the Manitoba Court of Queen's Bench said in a written judgment, on the case's appeal, that there was no general rule that parents were liable for offences committed by their children. As a result he ruled invalid the attempt by Zellers Inc. to collect from the woman.[10]

Zellers' lawyer Todd Hewett declared, "I don't think the case will have any broad-brush effect on the nation-wide recovery program." The demand letter the woman received read "Should you elect to ignore this demand, refuse or fail to pay the amount of the proposed out-of-court settlement, Zellers will take the case before a civil court and claim legal damages." Officials for the retailer testified they had not taken anyone to court despite issuing hundreds of threats. Usually the demand was for $325 but the mother was issued a bill for $225 because another boy was involved in the offence — whose mother also got a $225 demand letter. As a result of demand letters issued in the three years of its policy, Zellers and the Hudson's Bay department store chain (part of the same corporation) recovered over $1 million.[11]

The media attention to the Winnipeg case set off a storm of protest across the country against both Zellers and the Bay. Even if the stores succeeded with their policy at higher court levels it could ultimately backfire, if only because it could buy the retailers more bad publicity than it saved in settlements and prosecutions. Two women's groups in the province of Nova Scotia called for a nationwide consumer boycott of Zellers and the Bay because of the demand program, on the ground that the policy put people who had paid their debt to society in double jeopardy. They were punished once in court when the criminal charges were heard, and again by the stores that demanded payment. Zellers and the Bay took civil action as well as prosecuting shoplifters criminally. Brian Thomson, Zellers' spokesman, said revenue from the civil recovery payments covered only about five percent of the costs of maintaining store security and of apprehending and processing shoplifters. Said Katherine McDonald, president of the Nova Scotia Advisory Council on the Status of Women, "it amounts to extortion" and the payments demanded are "inappropriate, unethical, immoral" and far more than the costs of prosecuting offenders. Kathleen Jennex, executive director of Coverdale Court Work Services, a Halifax group that helped women in conflict with the law, termed the program "intimidating." In Ottawa, the Salvation Army voiced its concerns, as did several Toronto legal clinics. The process began when a store called in the police. Later, a letter was sent to the offenders — or parents — telling them that they could prevent a civil action by paying a "settlement amount." That was usually $325 but could be higher if the initial fine wasn't paid. If the offenders did not pay up, they got a second letter warning of court action, which was followed by a statement of claim. Salvation Army spokesperson Cathy Baril said, "The damages claimed are far in excess of those actually suffered. Stolen items are placed back on the shelf for sale and each case only occupies a security officer for an average of an hour — about $12. All the scheme does is line the pockets of those operating it and gives offenders the idea they can buy their way out of trouble." The Bay used a private company to collect on its demands, keeping $200 out of each $325 settlement. The collecting firm got $80 with the remaining $45 going to legal fees. Thomson said Zellers did not view its civil program in terms of profit for the store: "We are bringing to the forefront the awareness that if you are caught shoplifting at Zellers you are going to be asked to pay us back. This is a deterrent to make people think twice."[12]

Three strikes and you're out became popular statutes in America again in the 1990s. By the end of the decade, 38 states had some version of a three-strikes law that imposed stiffened sentences on repeat offenders. One of those states was California, which enacted a three-strikes law as a voter initiative in 1994. Under the law, three convictions meant the judge was required to impose a sentence of 25 years to life. One of the victims was Michael Riggs who received such a sentence for shoplifting a $20 bottle of vitamins. Riggs had not just two prior convictions, but eight, and had served prison time for offenses like car theft and robbery, all committed before the California law was enacted. The shoplifting offense that put Riggs away for a minimum of 20.8 years before parole eligibility would ordinarily have earned a maximum sentence of six months. In 1997, the California Supreme Court refused to hear his appeal even though it noted the offence was a petty theft motivated by homelessness and hunger. And even though it noted that Riggs had a drug abuse problem, apparently precipitated by the death of his young son, the appeals court indicated that Riggs had forfeited whatever sympathy his plight may have otherwise earned him because of his numerous prior convictions. Two years later the United States Supreme Court refused to hear his appeal although four justices agreed it raised serious questions.[13]

Ernst & Young surveyed 160 United States retailers in 1990, including department stores, drug stores, supermarkets, and specialty apparel shops. They found that the shrinkage rate was 1.91 percent in the United States in 1989, 1.88 percent in 1988, and 1.83 percent in 1987, that is, percentage at retail value. When priced at cost, shrinkage was 1.2 percent in both 1989 and 1988. The surveyed stores had total sales of $192.5 billion, with shrinkage thus equal to $3.7 billion. Extrapolating to all American retailers, excluding car dealers, the survey suggested shrinkage totaled over $20 billion. During 1989, the surveyed shopkeepers apprehended 638,054 customers and 49,916 employees in the act of stealing. Average value of merchandise or cash recovered was seven times higher among employees than among customers, $1,350 versus $196. That led the survey to decide employees accounted for 35 percent of the dollar volume of all shrinkage. Forty-six percent of respondents cited drug use as the biggest factor behind shoplifting, while 55 percent said it was at the root of employee theft. In the previous year only 42 percent cited drugs as a major cause of all thefts. Also, the survey found that 40 percent of all retailers were testing employees for drug use, up from 21 percent in the previous year.[14]

According to the FBI, in 1990 there were 1.2 million shoplifting incidents, known to the police, up from 1.1 million in 1989. Shoplifting then accounted for 16 percent of all reported larcenies. In this account shrinkage was put at two percent for an average department store with one-third of all shrinkage said to be due to shoplifting. Among reasons cited for the offense was "the growing number of drug-users who steal to support their habit."[15]

Writing in *Seventeen* magazine in early 1992, James Thornton said that shoplifting totaled $10 billion a year and that an average family of four would save over $1,000 a year if all shoplifting suddenly stopped. The main thrust of the article was about teenage girls who stole, and why. To make its moral case against the offence, it used exaggeration. For example, Thornton wrote that when a teenager is caught shoplifting he or she "is likely to be handed over automatically to the police." That was very far from reality.[16]

Business writer Joe Dacy III stated in November 1992 that shoplifters cost American business as much as $26 billion a year in stolen merchandise.[17]

A nationwide National Retail Security Survey in 1992 looked at data provided by 477 retail firms who reported an overall shrinkage rate of 1.91 percent, in 1991, compared to 1.79 percent in 1990. Those companies attributed 38.4 percent of their losses to shoplifting, 37.8 percent to employee theft, 18 percent to paperwork errors, and 5.8 percent to vendor fraud or error. In an effort to limit their losses, 34.6 percent of those retailers reported using honesty shoppers, 30.1 percent used electronic article surveillance systems, and 35.7 percent used closed-circuit television systems. With regard to detection of shoplifters, regular employees were credited with 71 percent of the pilferers, 15.9 percent more were detected by security employees, 10.3 percent were discovered by electronic article surveillance systems, and customer tip-offs were credited with 2.9 percent of shoplifter detection. Regarding employee theft detections, 43.3 percent were attributed to coworker tip-offs, security audits were responsible for

24.7 percent, other reports accounted for 18.5 percent, honesty shoppers were responsible for 8.1 percent, and electronic article surveillance systems accounted for another 5.3 percent. Retailers who had compensation levels 10 percent or more higher than their competitors reported shrinkage rates that were approximately 30 percent lower. When both full- and part-time employees were eligible for profit sharing, shrinkage was reported to be 25 percent lower than at retailers which did not offer profit sharing to their employees. Stores that had sales clerk turnover rates of less than 10 percent reported an average shrinkage rate of 1.6 percent, compared with rates of approximately 2.5 percent at companies with sales clerk turnover of more than 91 percent.[18]

A year later, the same survey, conducted by the University of Florida, determined the shrinkage rate for 1992 to be 1.88 percent of sales.[19]

When William Ecenbarger did a general article on the problem in the June 1996 issue of *Reader's Digest*, he reported that shoplifters were "part of a growing army of Americans" who cost retailers $10 to $12 billion annually. And that didn't include the reported $7 to $10 billion that had been spent in the previous year in an effort to prevent shoplifting. Such offenses had more than doubled in the previous 20 years, he wrote, and the average American household paid $200 a year in higher prices because of shoplifting. Some 15 percent of all offenders were classed by him as professionals. The American Psychiatric Association was cited as saying that fewer than five percent of shoplifters were kleptomaniacs—"people who can't resist the impulse to steal." According to Ecenbarger about 98 percent of all shoplifting was successful because, of the estimated 60 million pilfering incidents in the previous year, only 1.2 million were detected. Asking the question, "What did shoplifting say about America?" the author replied to his own question by stating that it was just another form of the search for wealth without work, like income tax and expense account cheating. Read Hayes, president of the security consulting firm Loss Prevention Specialists, stated, "Shoplifting is a direct manifestation of the moral relativism in our society. Everyone knows it's wrong to take something without paying — that's why shoplifters feel a need to rationalize the act."[20]

Results from the 1997 National Retail Security Survey conducted by the Security Research Project of the University of Florida stated that retail companies lost a total of $26.2 billion to shrinkage in 1996, or 1.81 percent of sales, down from the 1995 level of 1.87 percent and below the high of 1.95 percent recorded in 1994. They also found that employee theft was again the largest source of shrinkage, representing an estimated 41 percent of the total; shoplifting accounted for 35.5 percent with all "other" responsible for 23.5 percent of the total.[21]

A 1998 study, Retail Theft Trend Reports, conducted by Orlando, Florida–based Loss Prevention Specialists and funded by Boca Raton, Florida–based Sensormatic Electronics Corporation said that United States retailers lost $9 billion annually to shoplifting. It added that the gender split for pilferers was 55/45 in favor of males, that more than one-third of the incidents involved teenagers—more than their representation in the general population—and that topping the list of stolen articles were tobacco products, athletic shoes, and designer jeans. Saturday was the most popular day to shoplift, recording 18 percent of the incidents, with Sunday the least favorite at 13 percent. Favorite time of the day to pilfer remained, as always, 3:00 to 6:00 P.M., with 34.2 percent of the incidents, next was noon to 3:00 P.M. at 25.9 percent, then 6:00 to 9:00 P.M. at 23.5 percent.[22]

At police seminars held in Connecticut in December 1998 to help retailers prepare for the Christmas rush of shoplifters, Westport police told the store owners that there were five general types of shoplifters; the amateur, the professional, the juvenile, the drug addict, and the kleptomaniac. In explaining shoplifting, John Jay Rouse, assistant professor of criminal justice at Sacred Heart University said, "Shoplifting is impossible to eradicate.... It's how people make their living. Shoplifters are very sophisticated. They have no desire to have a regular job. It's their way to earn money. They seek high quality clothing that they can get a good cash return. Some is shipped overseas."[23]

Canadian retailers were reportedly losing $6 million a day through shrinkage. According to the survey of 202 retailers by the Retail Council of Canada, median shrinkage was 1.5 percent for 1990, up from the 1.28 percent found in the 1989 study, which covered only 145 stores. Supposedly the $6 million a day ($2 billion per year) was twice what it was two years earlier. Of the total amount, $3 million was said to be due to shoplifting, $1.5 to $2 million due to employee theft, while accounting mistakes made up $1 to $1.5 million. Highest median shrinkage rate was 2.2 percent at family clothing stores, down to supermarkets at 0.25 percent. Twenty-six percent of responding retailers reported no continuing security expenses designed to stop thievery but 26.8 percent reported security expenses equaling at least 0.51 percent of total sales. Retailers who prosecuted all employees caught stealing (in addition to firing them) totaled 28.7 percent while 38.6 percent prosecuted all shoplifters. About 52 percent of the stores said they prosecuted, in both categories, on a case-by-case basis. The remainder did not prosecute any, of either group.[24]

The following year the Retail Council of Canada announced the shrinkage rate was 1.8 percent for 1991, although they said shrinkage still amounted to $2 billion a year.[25]

In Canada anyone could arrest without a warrant a person they had "personally observed" committing an indictable offense. However, only the police could arrest on "reasonable and probable grounds" a person suspected of having committed a crime. The former was a citizen's arrest. An arrest wasn't ordinarily performed in Canada until the suspect left the store.[26]

For 1993 the Retail Council of Canada put the median shrinkage rate at 1.4 percent. The newspaper carrying the account added that customers were stealing to the tune of $6 million a day when, in fact, the shrinkage total represented all losses. The Retail Council itself put the shoplifting loss at $3 million per day.[27]

When the Council released its 1995 report early in 1996, the group said the shrinkage rate was 1.95 percent for 1995, compared to 1.84 percent in 1994. Total loss was said to be $4 billion in 1995, up from $3 billion the previous year. The Council's survey was completed by 141 retailers in 23 sectors, across Canada. Shoplifters reportedly took $6 million a day, employee theft $3 million a day. Canadian retailers were said to be ready to start playing a more active role in processing pilferers they caught under a new policy developed with the Canadian Association of Chiefs of Police. In some cases the police may decide not to send an officer to the store. In such situations, retailers would complete a report that would be forwarded to the police, who would then lay charges. That approach was left to the discretion of the police. Said council president Diane Brisebois, "The retail council fully endorses the [new policy] and we look forward to continuing to work with the police to reduce store crimes of all kinds."[28]

From the UK, *The Economist* magazine reported that shrinkage amounted to about 2 billion pounds Sterling in 1991, one percent of retail sales, and that the total was growing at the rate of roughly 15 percent a year. According to statistics released by the Home Office, up to 80 out of every 1,000 people who went into a shop would steal from it. Police in London's busy West End estimated that only one in five of the people apprehended by stores for shoplifting were ever handed over to them.[29]

Data from a survey of retail outlets in the UK for 1990 indicated that 61,106 people were apprehended that year for shoplifting: 50.7 percent were males, 49.3 percent were females. Those aged under 10 made up 2.2 percent of those caught; 10- to 16-year-olds were 24.7 percent; 17- to 29-year-olds made up 38.4 percent of those caught; 30- to 59-year-olds were 24.3 percent; and those 60 and older comprised 10.4 percent. Those under 30 years of age made up 65.3 percent of those apprehended, a total that was close to American figures.[30]

One of the more interesting events was a shoplifting sting operation set up in Chicago. In May 1988, Lew Shealy was vice president of loss prevention for Marshall Field department store in Chicago. Worried about shoplifting, he approached the FBI and the sheriff of Cook County and outlined a sting operation. With the FBI's blessing, Sheriff James O'Grady agreed to help. Shealy recruited four other retailers to join Marshall Field in bankrolling the operation. Together they put in $30,000 and rented a storefront in a Chicago suburb. Then the retailers contributed store fixtures and inventory (all apparel). Next, five Cook County detectives were brought in for training; they learned how to operate the store and its closed-circuit television system. They opened under the name J & O Clothiers (for James O'Grady) and quickly became known in the area as a place to sell stolen merchandise. One reason it became so popular so quickly was that the police were paying 30 cents on the dollar when purchasing pilfered items—others were paying 25 cents. The store operated for 18 months. Bags with foil liners (to deflect electronic article surveillance systems) were popular tools used by pilferers, as was the tactic of carrying booster boxes—empty cartons wrapped up like gifts, with false bottoms. Some 45 shoplifters were indicted by the Cook County Grand Jury and 13 of those were jailed. Reportedly around $1 million in stolen merchandise was recovered and that real fencing operations were also shut down, leading to the recovery of an additional $1 million worth of articles.[31]

Psychological profiles and explanations continued to appear in women's magazines. In its February 1992 issue, *Good Housekeeping* profiled a 45-year-old woman in a piece titled, "I Was a Shoplifter." Her daughter had married and moved away, her husband worked late, she had just quit her job to devote more time to herself and her husband but found herself bored, her life empty, no purpose, and so on. She took to shoplifting. Finally caught, she was sentenced to a rehabilitation program with Shoplifters Anonymous. In the course of that program she discovered the underlying reasons for her pilfering. She and her husband went for marriage counseling through which even more hidden problems were unearthed. But it all worked out, said the woman: "Maybe Ken and I needed that terrible time to draw us together. We're closer than ever today." It was a tale full of great moral uplift with everything rooted in individual deficiencies and no mention made of retailers' responsibility in impulse generation.[32]

McCall's magazine profiled female shoplifters in its May 1995 number, women for whom "hostility is frequently at the root of the crime.... Shoplifting is really a lashing out." Featured was a woman who began shoplifting when her husband left her and their three children. Another woman piled up her pilfered loot at home in boxes. She was so fearful of discovery that she wouldn't let her adult children visit. The question those women needed to ask themselves was, said the article, "What need in my life is not being met?" The closest the piece came to displaying insight was in the statement, "Indeed, some blame society's 'look good, feel good' motto and the unrealistic standards of beauty imposed by the media for practically driving women to break the law." Articles such as these all had their roots in an era when shoplifting was predominantly a female crime (or perceived as such) and the reasons could be looked for in the place of women in a patriarchal society. As well, all had some grounding in a kleptomaniac environment; even though the term itself was not used. However, the sex division within shoplifting was around 50/50 and had been for decades, and perhaps longer. Male shoplifters were never profiled in the media the way women were. For that matter they were not profiled at all. Even that much earlier, preponderance of women pilferers may have been more artifact than real — a function of the fact that females comprised up to 90 percent of all shoppers.[33]

One of the more unusual cases began the day after Thanksgiving in 1996 when 37-year-old Gregory Thomas — who had served time in prison for theft — was arrested for shoplifting. He told the police a tale in which he claimed to have been a hired shoplifter for the upscale Dick family which lived in a suburb of St. Paul, Minnesota. Over the years he claimed to have shoplifted more than $250,000 worth of goods for them. Thomas agreed to take part in a sting operation in which he and an undercover cop, posing as a department store cleaner, went to the Dick home, sold them some goods, and took their order for future goods to be shoplifted. In December 1996 the four-member Dick family was charged with receiving stolen goods.[34]

Authors whose works were shoplifted most often from New York City bookstores in late 1997 were Vladimir Nabokov, Thomas Pynchon, Charles Bukowski, Paul Aster, Albert Camus, Raymond Carver, Cormac McCarthy, Henry Miller, Jim Thompson, and William S. Burroughs. Reporter Edward Lewine said that the theme that united them was "a strong anti-establishment bent. These are writings that appeal to a sense of protest." Worrying to some was that the taste of the thieves, and the people they sold to, was almost exclusively for 20- or 30-year-old books which "seems to signal a terrible poverty of contemporary letters." Of the names on the list, only three — Auster, McCarthy and Pynchon — were then alive. Lewine wondered if the taste reflected by the thieves was the taste of Americans in general or simply of those who stole.[35]

When the *Times* published another article on the topic 18 months later, Joyce Jensen reported that top picks for shoplifters on both coasts were the works of the Beat poets Jack Kerouac, Allen Ginsberg, William S. Burroughs, and Charles Bukowski. Right behind the Beats came the Bible. Over in Britain, Jack Kerouac was said to top the same list.[36]

One report, in the unlikely source *National Petroleum News*, said that according to several security experts shoplifting represented a very small portion of overall shrinkage, amounting to perhaps no more than five percent of a store's cash and merchandise losses on average. It was said to be so low because employee theft was said to be so high. Many oil companies were then heavily involved in running convenience stores as adjuncts to their gas bars.[37]

Throughout the 1990s the Retail Council of Canada maintained that shoplifting was responsible for about 50 percent of the total shrinkage loss with employee theft and paperwork error making up the remainder. For the year 1994, the group estimated Canadian retailers had shrinkage of $3 billion with shoplifters taking $1.5 billion, employees $900 million, and paperwork and bookkeeping errors the other $600 million. On average, the Council reported, a shoplifter took $82 worth of items each time while an employee made off with $203 worth of articles in each incident.[38]

Retailers continued to try a variety of methods to lessen shoplifting. In Idaho around 1990, the Boise Police Department and local retail security personnel began a co-op effort. Program features included monthly meetings held for retail security and law enforcement personnel to exchange information on known shoplifters and fraudulent refunders— that is, people who pilfered goods which they then brought back to the outlet in an attempt to obtain a refund. According to the account, "refund information is examined to develop potential suspects and get current addresses for law enforcement use. Retailers can use information from other stores to place suspects on a 'no-refund' status." Also, picture bulletins were distributed to police and security personnel so they could recognize suspects as they entered businesses. Curt Crum, director of the Boise Police Department's Business Crime Watch, noted, "Our guidelines allow pictures to be distributed only on suspects with prior theft-related convictions."[39]

The Real Canadian Superstore in Vancouver, BC — part of a chain of huge discount outlets— had for several years instructed their employees to conduct checks for shoplifted goods, including searching bags and backpacks, as customers exited the store. That policy of random search earned the store almost universal condemnation in newspapers and on television after a customer went to the media in 1991. He declined to be searched and was followed to his car by a security guard. British Columbia Civil Liberties Association president John Westwood considered the policy to

be offensive: "It's an abuse of power." The customer was under no oblig-
ation to cooperate because random searches, by definition, do not have
"reasonable and probable grounds." The large supermarket chain, Canada
Safeway, did not conduct any random searches. Vice president of public
affairs for that company, Jim Waters, said they didn't perform searches
because "you're sending a signal to the customer that's very negative. Most
shoppers are honest, and will be quite resentful of any suggestion otherwise." Under the Canadian Charter of Rights and Freedoms, a search could
be considered unreasonable if it was shown to have been conducted without probable cause to believe that a criminal offense had been committed.
Nevertheless, Superstore said it had no plans to discontinue its search policy.[40]

Rehabilitation programs continued to play a minor role in the war
on shoplifting. Typical of such programs was Stoplift, set up in 1981 by a
nonprofit organization, Education and Assistance Corporation. Intended
to reduce recidivism, it was a program for beginning shoplifters which
served Nassau, Suffolk, and Queens in New York State. Stoplift's partners
in development were the State Department of Criminal Justice, the State
Department of Education and the Retail Loss Prevention Association — an
organization of major retailers. Eligible for the program were first and second time shoplifting offenders. When reporter Susan Konig profiled Stoplift in 1996 she did so against the background that shoplifting was the
nation's most expensive crime, accounting for monetary losses of $16 bil-
lion each year. People taken into the program took a 6-hour Saturday class
(for which they paid $85) in which they were asked to examine the motives
for their crime, to learn the legal consequences of continued shoplifting,
and to analyze the cost, both to themselves and to society at large. Six
months after completing the program — if no other criminal convictions
were made against them — their fingerprints were mailed back to them
and the incident was removed from the records. During class, the instructors answered the question as to what made a shoplifter by saying, "Relative deprivation.... A psychological condition where one feels left out of
the bounty of the marketplace." Stressed by instructors was the role of
impulse — that pilfering was usually not planned out. New York State protected its retailers through the Merchant's Privilege Statute and, said
instructor Alan Sirowitz, "They don't have to Mirandize you — read you
your rights. They can manhandle you, spill out your bags or your purse,
pretty much do what they want. A lot of people think that's unfair and
think it should be changed. But right now, it's the law." Nearly all of the
people in the program said they had shoplifted before, and none said they
would consider it again.[41]

However, most of the effort by retailers to thwart pilferers was directed toward the electronic article surveillance systems. Stores didn't want to rehabilitate shoplifters, or charge them in the first place. What they wanted was to deter it to stop it from happening in the first place. It meant they needed a more daunting, more intimidating EAS system. As the 1990s began, retailers were starting to get excited by the latest development in EAS — source tagging. In source tagging, the security circuit was embedded in a product or in the product packaging at the point of manufacture. The ability to place more merchandise out in the open without security worries would encourage impulse sales, as customers would be able to touch, examine, and purchase products with little or no sales assistance. Supposedly, an average of 40 percent of all purchases were made on impulse. However, statistics showed that self-service merchandising increased shrinkage. Source tagging would also eliminate tagging labor at the retail level. Elimination of tagging labor, increased impulse sales, and reduced security worries were some of the obvious benefits that excited retailers. Reporter Gerald Klein observed that "self-service merchandising and impulse sales are the two main forces driving the concept of source tagging."[42]

Ross Stores was involved in 1991 in a pilot program with Checkpoint to implement source tagging in its earring cards. Checkpoint set up its Impulse program, a source tagging program that held its first industry conference in February 1991 to investigate the possibilities of source tagging. It functioned under the acronym IDEAS (Industry Direction on Electronic Article Surveillance). One benefit to manufacturers was that source tagging was seen as a way for manufacturers whose goods were usually kept behind locked cases to enable their products to be sold in more open displays on the retail selling floor. Part of the strength of source tagging was that pilferers would not be able to easily determine the location of the tag, or which products were protected and which were not. Neither would employees, so a bulk deactivation unit was needed and used as part of a source tagging system.[43]

Between 1987 and 1991 Sensormatic sales revenue increased from $95 million to $239 million, more than its two closest competitors combined, Checkpoint and Knogo. In 1990 Sensormatic collected $14 million from industrial customers, and hoped to reach $100 million by 1995. Those customers were buying such things as closed-circuit television systems and electronic identification door openers to monitor employees. One reason for the large increase in Sensormatic sales was a technology that used magnetic fields instead of radio waves. Metal or magnetized objects such as canned goods or even credit cards sometime set off false alarms when shoppers passed through gates that emitted radio waves. During the 1980s retailers used tags to protect mostly clothing, books, pharmaceuticals, and recorded music. Increasingly they were found in dozens of shapes and sizes, on eyeglasses, telephones, newborn babies (53 had been stolen from maternity wards from 1983 to 1991), wallpaper-sample books, oil paintings, health-club towels, fax machines, and patients with Alzheimer's disease, who might wander off hospital premises.[44]

Articles continued to show that EAS systems were catching on in the supermarket industry. Yet, by mid–1993 estimates were that supermarket penetration by EAS systems was less than five percent of stores. By this time a fourth major EAS provider was in the field, 3M Shoplifting Control Systems. All the companies relied on magnetic field technology to trigger the alarms except for Checkpoint, which used radio frequency. Checkpoint had the most supermarket installations, about 3,000, while Sensormatic had about 700. While the supermarket industry was still interested in source tagging, with less than five percent penetration, it had little clout. Another major problem for source tagging was the question of standards; with four different systems in use, how was the industry to establish source tagging with just one standard? A source tagging system which would set off an alarm going through a Sensormatic gate would have no effect going through the gates of the other three systems, and so forth.[45]

When journalist Scott Dawson reviewed the state of the EAS industry in the fall of 1993, he did so against a background in which he estimated annual losses from shoplifting in 1990 at $50 billion and observed that retail entities were increasingly large national chains "that frequently rely on self-service and have exceptional rates of personnel turnover." Some people felt less guilty about stealing from stores that seemed more distant and more impersonal. For Dawson, EAS systems had two major drawbacks. One was that they were not a deterrent to employee theft, "which according to retail security professionals is the major source of shrinkage volume." However, the most serious problem was "consumer ill will caused by false alarms." Most probable cause of that was from store personnel not deactivating the sensitized tag on purchased merchandise. A 1984 New York City case was brought by a shopper who claimed to have been mistreated after triggering an EAS alarm, caused by a clerk who failed to remove a sensor device. The court awarded the customer a total of $175,000 in both compensatory and punitive damages. Evidence from this case showed that the retailer had been making about 100 erroneous stops per week. When a random sample of 250 people were given questionnaires, it was learned that a substantial proportion of respondents, 42 percent, had accidentally set off an EAS alarm, and five percent had set off an alarm four or more times. Another question on the survey asked the respondents what their reaction would be to setting off an EAS alarm. Thirty-eight percent said they would shop less at the store in the future; 74 percent would expect an apology and an explanation from the store manager; 16 percent said they would never shop at the store again.[46]

Target stores tried a test within their chain. In a Detroit outlet, a type of calculator had a tag embedded and was openly displayed for customers to help themselves. At an Indianapolis store, the item was openly displayed but did not have a tag embedded in it. Finally, in a Target outlet in the Minneapolis area, tagged calculators were kept in a glass case that could be opened only by the sales clerk. Said King Rogers, vice president of loss prevention for Target, "In the market where it was tagged and accessible, the sales rate was much greater and shortage was virtually nonexistent." Commenting on the battle going on over source tagging Rogers said "few manufacturers would proceed with source tagging until a vast majority of the retail community agreed on a standard." A spokesman for battery maker Duracell Inc., James Donahue, said that some of the largest customers of his company did not regard source tagging as a meaningful solution because much of the shrinkage that occurred was due to employee theft. "They believe the product isn't walking out with their customers. And their employees are obviously familiar enough with the system to find a way around it."[47]

Nonetheless, attempts to adopt a source tag continued, which led to a major fight between Sensormatic (sales of $310 million in 1992) and Checkpoint (1991 sales of $72 million), each of which wanted its standards adopted by source taggers. The battle included charges of false advertising, bad faith, and irresponsible disclosures. Christopher Brown, a market development manager at Sensormatic said, "The level to which the current discussion has dropped is an embarrassment to our industry." Sensormatic's system involved tags using "acousto-magnetic" signals to sound warnings while the Checkpoint system continued to use radio frequencies to set off alarms. When the National Association of Recording Merchandisers (NARM) studied the various systems, before recommending to its 850 members which anti-theft system to use, Checkpoint took the offensive by placing a full-page ad in an issue of *Billboard* magazine. It cited two independent studies that indicated that deactivating acousto-magnetic tags distorted the audio quality of recorded music, which would make the technology unacceptable to recording merchants. Sensormatic responded with a $35 million lawsuit.[48]

Checkpoint's tags were less expensive than those of Sensormatic but were said to be notorious for setting off false alarms. Many retailers would rather suffer some shrinkage than fight an array of wrongful arrest lawsuits. Sensormatic's system needed two unique signals, acoustic and magnetic, to set it off, making it nearly free of false alarms. In its campaign to win NARM's favor, Sensormatic said it was approached by a drug store chain that had already paid out over $1 million in false arrest claims stemming from false alarms triggered by Checkpoint systems.[49]

In March 1993, NARM recommended to its 6,000 member stores that they use the Sensormatic system to protect their recorded music stock. The trade group cited several reasons. For one, cash registers, radio frequencies and television monitors did not interfere with that system. Sensormatic tags were more expensive than Checkpoint's labels, about 6 cents versus 3 to 4 cents. The cost had been usually absorbed by the retailers but would be shifted to the manufacturers if source tagging became the norm. Within a couple of months of NARM's decision, the manufacturers' group, the Recording Industry Association of America, announced it had stepped in to re-examine the choice of the recording merchants.[50]

At the time of NARM's decision, Sensormatic had 70 percent of the antishoplifting security market, Knogo had 12 percent, and Checkpoint had nine percent. NARM chose Sensormatic's system (called UltraMax) on condition that the company agree to license its technology to competitors for a reasonable royalty. Standing number two in Europe, Sensormatic had just purchased ALP, the largest distributor and servicer of antishoplifting equipment in Europe.[51]

Sonopress, the manufacturing division of the Bertelsmann Music Group of Germany announced in spring 1993 that it had selected two Knogo theft-detection products that would be embedded directly into recorded material such as cassette tapes and compact discs. Knogo had argued that getting manufacturers to apply tags to packaging was only a stop-gap solution. The company contended that thieves could simply remove the anti-theft tags from packages and that embedded devices were more effective. Sensormatic's system embedded into packaging, not the item.[52]

For 1995 Sensormatic had revenues of $995 million and 65 percent of the worldwide electronic security market, while Checkpoint came in second with sales of $205 million. That same year, wrote business reporter Jill Sieder, United States retailers lost an estimated $30 billion to theft by employees and customers, an 11 percent increase since 1991. Home Depot, a $15 billion retailer, had by then persuaded more than 100 of its suppliers, including Stanley Tools and Black & Decker, to source tag using the Sensormatic system. It was cheaper for retailers and harder for a thief to remove or defeat such tags. As a result items that used to be locked up behind glass or chained down in the Tool Corral, such as $149 gas-powered leaf blowers, could be displayed in the open. Retailers believed that such open displays led to more sales. Each of the two main technologies had its detractors. Sensormatic supporters argued that Checkpoint's radio frequency misfired too often, creating false alarms. Checkpoint fans claimed Sensormatic scanning equipment could wreak havoc on the magnetic strips of music cassette tapes, credit cards and telephone cards. Sieder concluded by stating that because retailers pass on the cost of theft to honest shoppers, consumers get stuck paying as much as 15 percent more for certain goods, even though earlier in the piece she had said that shrinkage was two percent.[53]

Sensormatic's UltraMax system was a key part of the company's Universal Product Protection source tagging program. The marriage of source tagging and open merchandising was a retailer's dream. Apparel source tags also opened the door to comprehensive floor-ready merchandise programs. Floor-ready goods were items that had been priced, ticketed, and tagged before they arrived at the store.[54]

A medical study presented in May 1997 showed that Sensormatic's antishoplifting systems changed the heart rate of 49 out of 50 people wearing pacemakers. The company did not try to rebut the study but in a letter to retail stores that had in total purchased over 90,000 UltraMax detection systems, it said not to worry. Agreeing that UltraMax could alter the heartbeats of some customers entering and leaving the stores, Sensormatic said that it wasn't "clinically relevant." Although NARM continued to recommend the use of Sensormatic's UltraMax anti-theft devices with cassette tapes, the Academy of Country Music said they damaged music quality. Reportedly, Disney, the motion picture studio, was said to feel they hurt picture quality on its videos.[55]

Around 1995 there were still three companies in the antishoplifting system contest. Knogo North America was flogging its magnetic technology, Sensormatic had its acousto-magnetic system and Checkpoint had its radio frequency technology. The real prize was said to be the sale of tags, for which unit sales annually ran into the billions in the United States alone. Some analysts had suggested that vendors were all but giving that equipment away to retail accounts in order to establish a strong foothold for their systems. In any case, the suppliers had signed licensing agreements among themselves so that each would have access to the market should one technology become an industry standard. Knogo North America emerged as a company only in December 1994 after Sensormatic bought the international business of what had been Knogo Corporation. Knogo

North America continued to manufacture, sell, and service what had been
Knogo Corporation's EAS equipment in the United States and Canada.[56]

At the beginning of the 1990s, 1,692 survey questionnaires were given
to Georgia students in grades 7 through 12. Of the total, 632 (37 percent)
had shoplifted at least once in the previous year. Of those who self-reported
themselves to be shoplifters, 63.6 percent were male, 36.4 percent female.
In the nonshoplifting group 48.3 percent were male, 51.7 percent female.
Also cited was another study which found that 60.7 percent of shoplifters apprehended in three department stores were women. However, a second study found that 67 percent of all department store shoppers were
female.[57]

A different study gave out questionnaires to nine middle schools and
high schools in the southeastern United States. Completed surveys were
received from 780 males and 754 females. A total of 956 (62.3 percent)
were nonshoplifters; 219 (14.3 percent) stole only candy; 177 (11.5 percent)
either stole only one item other than candy or stole several relatively inex-
pensive items, such as school supplies and books; 182 (11.9 percent) stole
multiple items, including expensive products. The researchers in this study
commented that some retailers employed a second strategy of media and
school campaigns to discourage shoplifting, especially by adolescents. Such
campaigns had been sponsored by the National Retail Merchants Association, and the Retail Bureau of Metropolitan Washington D.C., as well as
retail trade groups in at least seven states. These researchers questioned
whether retailers had sufficient understanding of shoplifting's causes to
design such campaigns effectively. They believed that shoplifting spread
through peer influence (not so much through daring)— my friend does it,
he's okay, therefore shoplifting is alright. Exposure to shoplifting peers
tended to weaken the adolescent's own moral restraints against shoplifting. Also believed by the experimenters was the idea that a strong attach-
ment to parents decreased a youth's involvement in shoplifting by
bolstering the youth's acceptance of norms against this behavior and by
decreasing a youth's interaction with peers who shoplifted.[58]

A study done in the mid–1990s in Sweden looked at increased sales
and thefts of candy as a function of sales promotion activities. Conducted
in a grocery store in that country, researchers selected 20 candy products
and broke them into four groups of five items each. Variables tested were
price reduction and increased exposure (10 percent off, red sales tags on
shelves, regular shelf placement, and on a floor rack); price reduction alone
(10 percent off, red signs, regular shelf placement); increased exposure
alone (regular price, placement as in the first condition); control group
(regular price and placement). Items sold and disappeared were counted

in biweekly inventories for a two and one-half week baseline period, then a two-week intervention period, then a two-week baseline period again. In the condition of reduction in price and increased exposure, mean sales per week doubled, while in the 10 percent price reduction condition, mean sales increased 28 percent. In the increased exposure condition, mean sales increased by 35 percent; in the control condition, mean sales decreased by 12 percent. In the combined condition, thefts increased initially, from a mean of 13.6 thefts per week to a high of 51, and then declined. For this group alone, thefts increased for each product. In the 10 percent price reduction condition, thefts increased 90 percent while in the increased exposure group, thefts rose by 12.5 percent. For the control condition, thefts decreased from 12 to 5 per week. The experiments noted that the combination of price reduction and increased exposure was associated with the greatest increase in thefts and concluded, "The results are important because they suggest that promotional activities may increase sales volume but reduce net profit due to increased theft."[59]

A study by Ohio State University sociology professor Richard Lundman found that department store security officers were more likely to arrest accused shoplifters who were poor. Researchers found that shoplifters who lived in middle- or upper-class neighborhoods more often were released from custody than suspects from low-income areas. Said Lundman, "Some of the actions of private corporate police are troublesome. These private officers treat rich and poor differently." Researchers examined the records of 556 shoplifting apprehensions from 1985 to 1987 at a mall branch of a national department store chain. They compared shoplifters released with those who were charged. Accused pilferers who scuffled with security officers were 23 percent more likely to be charged than those who surrendered peacefully. Suspects who did not live in the community were arrested more often than those who did. The more expensive the item stolen, the more likely the suspect would be prosecuted. For each one dollar increase in the retail value of the item stolen, the odds of arrest increased 7.8 percent. Lundman's research indicated that department store security officers were far less lenient than public police. Other studies had shown that public police arrested about 10 to 15 percent of those accused of minor crimes such as shoplifting. But private corporate police arrested nearly two-thirds of apprehended shoplifters, noted this account, "even though most had taken items worth very little, almost all were entirely polite in their interaction, and very few resisted." This article concluded that a major reason for the high arrest rate was probably due to the fact that shoplifting was the major focus of store security officers; "if they didn't arrest shoplifters they would have very little to do."[60]

During the 1990s, one of the main issues in shoplifting was the growing spread of civil recovery laws and the use of such laws by retailers. It had the potential to become a profit maker in its own right and allow stores to reclaim more of their shrinkage than perhaps the pilferers had actually taken. What held retailers back from fuller use of those statutes was the fear of bad publicity and a backlash from its customers. It became more and more apparent that shoplifters were responsible only for a minor part of retailer shrinkage, probably no more than one-third, perhaps a lot less. Despite that, and evidence that the shrinkage rate was fairly steady at about two percent and had been so for years, or decades, the media still indulged in the use of exaggerated numbers in some of its articles and still proclaimed a pilfering epidemic from time to time. There remained no specific gender differences in shoplifters. Those apprehended tended to be young, under 30, but that could have been due to the inexperience or clumsiness of teenage pilferers. Or, it could have been a function of store security observing adolescents more closely than any other group, as females had at one time been the focus of differential observation. Since all groups appeared to have a baseline pilfering rate greater than zero, any differential observation would yield the expected result and reinforce the concept of differential observation. EAS systems continued to spread and to turn up on an ever growing number of items. Retailers, and the security industry, were keen on introducing source tagging because the retailers could shift the cost of tagging to the manufacturers and the security industry because it meant an increase in business. However, progress was slow in source tagging because manufacturers were less keen to pick up those costs, even when the carrot of extra sales from more open displays was dangled in front of them. Also slowing down the pace was the security industry itself with the main rivals each using equipment of a different technical standard. Studies continued to demonstrate the problems of allowing private corporate police to carry out policing functions. Citizens confronted by such store security personnel found they had less rights and were more likely to be treated with bias, and less leniently than could be expected from public police.

· *Chapter 8* ·

CONCLUSION

Although shoplifting has existed for centuries it only became a serious problem for retailers from shortly after the Civil War onwards. Prior to that, the practice was infrequent and engaged in principally by member of the economic underclass. That it was infrequent was due to the limited retailing which existed, relative to current times; the small physical size of stores wherein the owner was usually to be found and wherein he could personally observe most of the activity; and to the fact that most articles for sale were not on open display. That is, a customer had to ask a clerk to bring him the item from around some barrier.

Toward the end of the 1800s and beyond, retailing changed dramatically. Because of the technological advances of the Industrial Age a much greater variety of goods was produced and put on the market for sale. Growing in tandem was the advertising industry charged with convincing consumers to acquire all these goods, and to acquire them on credit when cash was not available. Retailing outlets quickly became gigantic and just as quickly moved to the open display of goods. Those early department stores pitched themselves directly to women because it was the females who then did the vast majority of the shopping.

Thus the stage was set for an upsurge in shoplifting activity which, indeed, took place. Not surprisingly, the bulk of those apprehended were women. However, it was often attributed to some defect within women, rather than an expected mathematical outcome. Those perpetrators were soon treated in two separate ways. Women from the under class and lower income groups continued to be treated as common criminals, often drawing harsh prison sentences, as such women had been treated for centuries. The other treatment, handed out to upper- and middle-class women, the "respectable" class, had two aspects. Firstly, a lot of these females were released by the retailer with no further action — this happened to people in all classes, but to a lesser extent in the lower reaches. Sometimes, though, retailers believed they should prosecute all the shoplifters they caught, in hopes of deterrence, and that a too freely used release policy might encourage shoplifting. It meant that sometimes "respectable" women found themselves in court on shoplifting charges. That was unacceptable to society in general, at least its upper reaches, with the result that a new concept was born which exonerated respectable women from pilfering charges, but not women who were members of the lower depths. That concept was kleptomania. Although it largely disappeared by around the time of World War I, as other ways of dealing with the class issue took precedent, the term kleptomania was still heard now and then, even into the 1990s. No one who worked in retailing, from clerks, to security personnel, to floorwalkers, to managers, ever gave the concept any credence, either today or a century ago.

A more pervasive and lasting effect from that era is the idea that shoplifters were mostly women. It was true then, of course, in absolute numbers, but hardly any men went into department stores in, say, the 1880s. Proportionately, there may have been no gender differences in pilfering rates. What research has been done in that area indicates that shoplifting rates vary little across sex, age, ethnic background, and so forth. What does happen with regularity is that store security personnel spend a disproportionate amount of their observational time on preselected target groups, women, or teens, or Blacks. Since all groups have some pilfering rate greater than zero then at the end of a time period a policy of observing teens disproportionately will lead to more teen apprehensions, which will reinforce the original assumption, which will lead to even more observational time spent on teens, which will lead to.... It all became a self-fulfilling prophecy. Teenagers were portrayed as the pilferers presenting the greatest problem in the 1960s, but before that they rarely drew a mention. Had shoplifting really changed or was this just another example of the bad publicity that youths drew for so many reasons in the "Hippie" era?

Media accounts of shoplifting often gave widely and wildly conflicting numbers as to the amount of money lost each year by retailers to inventory shrinkage. Using higher numbers when no evidence existed to support them was necessary when a media account wanted to talk about a dramatic increase in the offence, or that it had reached "epidemic" proportions. And they often did. Yet the best evidence seems to be that shrinkage rates have remained in a very narrow range of about two percent of gross sales for many decades, or longer. Numbers of shoplifting cases known to the police were largely meaningless because so many people apprehended in stores were released without further action. Suppose a store apprehended 1,000 shoplifters over a period of time and handed over 30 percent to the police. Then official police records would show 300 cases. Suppose in the next time period the store adopted a tougher prosecution policy and handed 40 percent over to the police, but apprehended only 900 people. Then 360 cases would be known to the police. In this example there was a decrease of ten percent in the incidence of shoplifting but the police would report it as a 20 percent increase. Reason enough for the media to do a story on the dramatic increase in shoplifting?

Whatever number was used for the annual losses due to shrinkage, all too often the media described it as goods lost to shoplifters. This was the case in recent times and a century ago as well. Yet taking a much bigger share of the goods were the other two factors involved in shrinkage: employee theft, and a general "other" category which included such things as honest and dishonest retailer recordkeeping errors and honest and dishonest errors by goods' suppliers. If a media account put the annual shrinkage loss to American retailers at $10 billion it was usually all too ready to state or imply that the $10 billion was lost to shoplifters. However, the best estimates would seem to put shoplifting's part in the loss at a top figure of 30 to 33 percent, $3.3 billion in this example.

Technology has been used more and more to combat the problem. It started with special mirrors and television cameras in the 1950s and moved on to the now ubiquitous sensitized tag and alarm gates. Its future, retailers hope, is source tagging, whereby the manufacturer will do all the work by embedding a tag directly into the product or its packaging during the manufacturing process. Nonetheless, during this period when retailers spent more and more money on gadgets to watch the goods and the customers, if media accounts were to be believed, shoplifting had continued to increase, sometimes dramatically. Of course, all of this high tech gadgetry had no effect whatsoever on the other causes of shrinkage, those that made up around two-thirds of the total. As well, during this period there was a shift in the type of employee responsible for store security. In earlier times the retailer hired his own staff for security functions. Today, though, more often than not those security people work for an outside firm, with whom the retailer contracts to provide security personnel. Their pay is lower, their benefits few, and the turnover rate is high. Moreover, the existence and prosperity of those private security firms is a function of the incidence of shoplifting, real or perceived. Those companies are part of a trend to move to a private justice system unaccountable to citizens at large. Suspects detained by private police have less rights than if they were detained by the public police; they are subjected to more erratic treatment and bias. As well, those private police make the determination of who will or will not be turned over to the public police for further action.

The enactment of laws by almost all states in the past few decades have made it easier for retailers, and private police, to deal with shoplifting suspects, and have left less recourse to those suspects. Laws initially established the right of retailers to detain suspects for a "reasonable" amount of time, to question them, to search them, and so forth, if everything was "reasonable." The next phase was the enactment of civil recovery statutes which allowed retailers to claim civil damages from shoplifting suspects, either instead of criminal prosecution, or in addition to it. This has often turned a case into little more than an extortion exercise and left private police regularly making the determination of whether or not to turn a detainee over to the public police solely on the grounds of the financial status of the suspect.

Retailers generally feel they get no sympathy on the issue, that people rarely feel any outrage in favor of the retailer when a person pilfers a $5 item from a giant faceless company. They prefer to believe they play no part in the event, except as blameless victims. Yet for decades now those retailers, and their advertising allies, have waged a never-ending campaign to get people to buy more, whether needed or not, whether wanted or not. More than a few retailers subscribe to an idea regarding the display of merchandise that goes something like this: if it isn't tempting enough to steal, it isn't tempting enough to buy. Stores release more of those they apprehend than they prosecute. It all reinforces the idea that shoplifting is not a serious crime; that it is not a real crime. One of the reasons stores lobbied long and hard, and successfully, for civil recovery laws was because they provided a way of getting money back from suspects without going through all the time delays and costs of public prosecution, and its attendant potential bad publicity. Retailers are content to let shoplifters be perceived as responsible for all the shrinkage since it takes the focus off the other, more important, factors. Shoplifting may present stores with a number of problems, but it is less difficult to deal with than the other factors.

While the media have treated us to a series of different images with regard to shoplifting, such as, the kleptomaniac, the housewife, the teenager, and the drug addict, the reality has more likely been that little has changed. If a particular group makes up 25 percent of the general population but supplies 60 percent of the customers for a particular retailer, then around 60 percent of those apprehended for pilfering at that retailer will likely come from that group.

NOTES

Chapter 1.

1. Elaine S. Abelson. "The invention of kleptomania." *Signs* 15, no. 1 (Autumn, 1989): 123; Mary Owen Cameron. *The Booster and the Snitch.* New York: The Free Press, 1964, p. 51.

2. "Conviction of a noted shoplifter." *New York Times*, April 28, 1865, p. 2.

3. "The Toombs—before Justice Hogan." *New York Times*, June 16, 1865, p. 8.

4. "Arrest of a notorious shoplifter." *New York Times*, February 19, 1874, p. 5.

5. "A gang of shoplifters broken up." *New York Times*, May 14, 1875, p. 5.

6. "Capture of a shoplifter." *New York Times*, February 16, 1876, p. 2.

7. "Two female shop-lifters arrested." *New York Times*, April 9, 1876, p. 2.

8. "Shoplifters arrested in Boston." *New York Times*, December 11, 1876, p. 5.

9. "An expert shoplifter arrested." *New York Times*, March 29, 1877, p. 8.

10. "A shoplifter's large pocket." *New York Times*, May 3, 1877, p. 2; "Shoplifter." *New York Times*, May 10, 1877, p. 2.

11. "Shoplifters convicted." *New York Times*, April 24, 1880, p. 3.

12. "Two Brooklyn shoplifters arrested." *New York Times*, December 24, 1877, p. 8.

13. "A shop-lifter of 'good character.'" *New York Times*, August 25, 1876, p. 8.

14. "Not guilty of shoplifting." *New York Times*, January 27, 1881, p. 3.

15. "Shop-lifting in Paris." *New York Times*, July 8, 1877, p. 10.

16. "Heavy raids by shop-lifters." *New York Times*, August 5, 1878, p. 1.

17. "Editorial." *New York Times*, May 28, 1878, p. 4.

18. "Wrongfully accused." *New York Times*, December 29, 1878, p. 12.

19. "A shoplifter convicted." *News York Times*, March 16, 1880, p. 3.

20. "Found guilty of shop-lifting." *New York Times*, August 6, 1879, p. 8.

21. "Current French topics." *New York Times*, May 11, 1878, p. 3.

22. "A kleptomaniac acquitted." *New York Times*, January 12, 1879, p. 8.

23. "The woman who pilfers." *New York Times*, May 31, 1878, p. 3.

24. Ibid.

25. "Romance in great shops." *New York Times*, January 14, 1883, p. 10.

26. "Pilfering from stores." *New York Times*, March 4, 1883, p. 5.

27. Ibid.

28. "Mrs. Martin's dual role." *New York Times*, April 11, 1895, p. 8.

29. "Store prisoner had $400." *New York Times*, April 11, 1905, p. 8.

30. "Shoplifting in New York." *New York Times*, January 2, 1906, p. 15.

31. "Holidays develop many shoplifters." *New York Times*, December 8, 1907, pt. 2, p. 5.

32. "30 shoplifters at once." *New York Times*, December 20, 1907, p. 1.

33. "War on shoplifters." *New York Times*, February 15, 1908, p. 3.

34. "Shoplifting in great department stores." *New York Times*, April 26, 1908, pt. 5, p. 8.

35. Ibid.

36. "Shop thefts of $1,000,000." *New York Times*, September 22, 1912, pt. 3, p. 6.

37. "War on shoplifters." *New York Times*, May 25, 1913, pt. 3, p. 5.

38. "Shoplifting loss $50,000." *New York Times*, January 25, 1914, sec. 2, p. 1.

39. Joy L. Santink. *Timothy Eaton and the Rise of his Department Store.* Toronto: University of Toronto Press, 1990, pp. 192–193.

40. Michael B. Miller. *The Bon Marche: Bourgeois Culture and the Department Store, 1869–1920.* Princeton, New Jersey: Princeton University Press, 1981, p. 197.

41. Elaine S. Abelson, op. cit., p. 137.

42. Ibid., pp. 137–139.

43. Ibid., pp. 136–137; William Ecenbarger. "They're stealing you blind." *Reader's Digest* 148 (June, 1996): 100.

44. Elaine S. Abelson, op. cit., pp. 123–124.

45. Ibid., pp. 124–125.

46. Patricia O'Brien. "The kleptomania diagnosis: bourgeois women and theft in late nineteenth-century France." *Journal of Social History* 17 (Fall, 1983): 65–66.

47. Ibid., pp. 70–71.

48. Michael B. Miller, op. cit., pp. 200–205.

49. Elaine S. Abelson, op. cit., p. 135; Patricia O'Brien, op. cit., p. 67.

50. Patricia O'Brien, op. cit., pp. 67–68.

51. Ibid., pp. 69, 71.

52. Ibid., pp. 71–72.

53. Emile Zola. *Au Bonheur des dames.* Paris, 1971, p. 277.

54. Elaine S. Abelson, op. cit., p. 136.

55. Ibid., pp. 125–126.

56. Ibid., p. 130.

57. Ibid., pp. 130–131.

58. Ibid., pp. 132–134.

59. Ibid., pp. 141, 143.

60. Rita Papazian. "For retailers, warnings on shoplifting." *New York Times*, December 13, 1998, Connecticut Sec., p. 5.

61. "Sleuthing for shoplifters." *The Literary Digest* 46 (April 26, 1913): 967.

62. "The husband who makes his wife a thief." *Ladies Home Journal* 32 (March, 1915): 16.

63. Elaine S. Abelson. *When Ladies Go A-Thieving: Middle-Class Shoplifters*